BEYOND
THE ASTRAL
METAPHYSICAL SHORT STORIES

WILLIAM BUHLMAN
SUSAN BUHLMAN

Print ISBN: 978-1-54397-265-8

eBook ISBN: 978-1-54397-266-5

TABLE OF CONTENTS

INTRODUCTION

We are an amazing nonphysical species using biological bodies for temporary experiences on Earth. The reality of our existence is far more interesting than the accepted concepts of body, mind and spirit. An exciting journey of self-exploration and discovery lies before us.

Open your mind to a more expansive vision. The true path to our spiritual essence/higher self is an inner journey of our consciousness beyond the physical body. This search requires the vision and courage to seek the invisible spiritual path that lies within us.

Some methods to travel the inner spiritual path are deep meditation, trance work, and self-initiated OBEs just to name a few. The key is for us to be completely open to an inner shift of our awareness from the outer physical to the subtle realms of consciousness within us.

This book provides unique stories of transformation written to enhance your connection to the inner journey of consciousness. We wish for you to enjoy these stories that speak to the highs and lows of our human adventure. Look carefully, you may see a reflection of your own physical journey as we relay our experiences to you.

Stretch your thoughts and see where your inspiration will take you!

THE BOY WHO COULD FLY

"Mom, I was flying last night, I'm not making it up!" Billy was ada-
mant. He had an incredible experience and had to make his point loud
and clear. He followed his mother around the kitchen trying to make her
understand. Anna stopped, put her dish towel on the counter, and grabbed
a bowl for his cereal. She looked him directly in the eyes and said, "Billy,
it was just a dream."

"No it wasn't Mom. It was real. I could see our neighborhood, my
school, and even Grandma's house!" Nothing she could say would dismiss
his excitement. He had entered a new world, but convincing her was going
to take some work.

"Son, dreams are your imagination at work while you sleep. We
can't really fly," she said as she poured corn flakes into the bowl in front
of him.

Billy appeared dejected as he slowly pushed his cereal around the
bowl. He couldn't understand why she wouldn't believe him. He expected
that from his teachers at school but not from his own mother.

"Billy, hurry and eat your breakfast—you don't want to miss
your bus."

He was disappointed as he thought to himself that adults just don't
get it.

This had been happening for some time. It was not unusual for Billy to be awakened in the middle of the night by strange vibrations, sounds, and numbness. On a few occasions he couldn't move his body at all and became afraid that there was something wrong with him. As more time passed, he began seeing through closed eyes and even felt as though his body was floating.

Those nights when his room appeared to have a soft moonlit glow, he floated up and hovered near the ceiling of his room. Imagining he was an astronaut suspended weightless in space helped to keep him calm. Once he got used to the floating sensations, he realized it was fun. Soon, he could easily swim around his room and even move through walls. He felt so free, it didn't even bother him that the wall color looked different and he couldn't read the words on his posters.

He tried to explain to his mother how real his night-time adventures were, but she didn't understand. She always called it a nice dream and said it would go away. Secretly, she wondered if he needed some medical attention. Maybe there was something wrong with his brain.

As the weeks progressed Billy continued his night-time explorations, each time discovering something new. Over time he saw that his thoughts were the sole engine that moved him. With practice, he found it easier to maintain his floating and flying by focusing on a single thing—a location or person. His thought control was important, because without it he would wander and then slip back into a dream or sleep. He prolonged his flights by pretending his physical body did not exist. His confidence and curiosity grew with each night time journey.

Then one night as he floated, he thought of flying like Superman and shot up through the ceiling at a terrifying speed. He was soaring so fast and high that it scared him; startled, he thought about his body and instantly snapped back into his room with a jolt. Once grounded, Billy was relieved to be in his bed again with no harm done.

Eventually 'Superman flying' became fun beyond words. He thought to himself, "Mom is not going to believe this. I bet night flying is where the entire idea of Superman came from." At school he excitedly told his friend Johnny about his night-time floating and flying, but his friend told him it sounded like an action figure dream, not a real experience. He felt so alone when even his best friend didn't believe him.

Lying in bed he thought of a way to prove to his mother his flying was real. Maybe he could see something unusual to convince her. That night the strange vibrations and sounds started again; Billy enjoyed the waves of energy moving through him. He surrendered to the vibrations and could feel himself become numb as he slowly moved away from his body, floating gently through the ceiling. In slow motion he glided through the rafters and the roof and hovered just above the top of the red-brick chimney. The ability to control his movement was increasing. Floating was such a subtle thing; adults could not begin to understand.

Silently suspended above the house he turned to look at his sur-roundings and could clearly see the green shingles of the roof. Focusing his vision he noticed a yellow round object in the gutter. It had to be a tennis ball. Excited by this discovery he snapped back to his body. The next morning at breakfast he told his mother about the ball in the gutter and how he had floated up and seen it. He was sure he had proof this time.

His mother just smiled and said, "Billy, you and your friends have thrown balls around the house. There are probably all kinds of toys on the roof." He felt dejected by her words; even evidence wouldn't make her believe!

After Billy left for school his mother pondered her son's strange stories. "I'm not sure what to do about his fantasy of flying. I wish that I could talk to someone about this, but I don't want anyone to think my son is crazy."

The next night Billy felt the familiar vibrations and drifted up through the roof. Hovering weightless over his house he slowly turned in space and decided to have some fun. Stretching out his arms he thought of flying and shot into the sky with incredible speed. This time he flew over his neighborhood; he could clearly see the playground and the baseball field at his school. After some time he began to get heavier and started to descend. While trying to maintain altitude he instead did a slow-motion crash landing to the ground and instantly snapped back into his body. Opening his eyes he smiled to himself; it didn't hurt, but he wondered why he had gotten so heavy. It was weird. Even so he felt proud of his flying and wished he could tell everyone about his amazing discoveries. He was excited but also frustrated; the entire world should know about this—what is wrong with the adults? They all seem so closed-minded.

One night he thought about the moon and instantly felt a sense of rapid motion. He was hovering just above the lunar surface. His vision cloudy, Billy spontaneously demanded, "Vision now!" Looking down he could see the gray craters of the moon. In the distance he could clearly see the Earth; it looked like a small, blue globe hanging in space. In awe, he realized the immensity of what he had experienced and he knew it was real. With a single thought of his body he was back in his bedroom pondering his experience. Then the reality sank in—no one is going to believe me. If my mother won't believe me, who will? Why don't adults know about this? If people knew they could fly, then all the stupid fighting in the world would stop. This could change everything!

Unknown to Billy, his mother was standing at his bedroom doorway. It was as if she needed to see for herself that her son had remained in his bed. When she was confident that he was not physically leaving his room, she finished folding the laundry and went to her own room. Maybe she should have a doctor look him over. "If there is someone who might have an answer for me, I'd really like some help," she said softly, not sure who was listening.

That night while Billy focused on his grandmother's house, he was surprised to see his dead grandfather instead. The kind man welcomed him warmly with his thoughts. "I am very impressed with you young man. You have become a very effective flyer!" Stunned by his abrupt appearance Billy responded, "Grand pop, I thought you were dead."

He smiled warmly. "No one ever dies; we just change our outer appearance. We stay the same inside."

"But you look so young."

"Yeah, that was a darn big surprise to me; everyone has a new body after they die. Our thoughts mold our appearance here. It's an amazing world we live in!"

"It is pretty amazing. Is this heaven?" Billy asked his grandfather.

"Billy, there are many different heavens. More than anyone can imagine. I've learned that life is just beginning at death. The choices available are beyond our imagination. The physical world is but a tiny part of the many worlds we live within."

"I have a lot to show you. Check this out!" In a flash, his grandfather appeared on a 1940s Indian motorcycle, complete with a sidecar.

Impressed by the sudden change, Billy couldn't contain his curiosity. "Wow, that's awesome, how did you do that?"

"Just focus your thoughts on a clear image in your mind and things become real. Once you learn the ropes in heaven it's a darn fun place. Come on, get in. Let's go for a ride." Billy climbed into the sidecar, got comfortable in his seat, and they took off for a drive in the mountains. Green, panoramic vistas unfolded with each turn.

"Where are we now?"

"We are cruising on the Skyline Drive in the mountains of Virginia. This was one of my favorite places to ride when I had a physical body. Nice name for this road, don't you think?"

"This is awesome," Billy said as he leaned left and right with the curves of the road. "Does everyone go to heaven?" he asked.

"Everyone continues, even animals. Most people are met by their loved ones and then rejoin them in their soul community. I was met by my mother—your great-grandmother—when I died."

"You said I was a flyer. Are there special heavens for flyers?" Billy had so many questions.

"There are many different walking and flying heavens, each created by the people who live there. The walkers limit themselves to a single heaven, but flyers are free to explore the many levels of heaven. As you have learned, flyers see beyond their eyes and don't accept the limits of the walkers. Flying is an essential skill in heaven because it gives you the freedom to do and see amazing stuff that walkers will never understand. Incredible teachers and schools exist in heaven; they teach people how to fly without limits." His grandfather pulled off to the side of the road to appreciate a breathtaking scenic overlook. Stepping off of his bike he gazed at the stunning view of mountain peaks projecting onto an endless blue sky. The pops of color from the spring blossoms on the surrounding bushes and trees were surreal.

"Grandpa, I have so much to learn."

"Yes, we all do. Soon you will learn the art of inner flight. This is where you learn to become a real explorer, an advanced flyer. This is how the answers to the big questions are found," said his grandfather as he returned his attention to his protégé.

"What big questions?" Billy asked.

"What are you? What is your purpose? Why do you exist? What is the meaning of life? Just to name a few. Flyers have the ability to discover the answers for themselves," said his grandfather as he led the boy to a picnic table seat.

"What do you mean?" Billy sat on the bench and hung on every word.

"There are many kinds of people in heaven; for example, there are walkers in heaven, just like on Earth; they remain content within their small world made of thoughts and beliefs. They see only with their eyes and don't seek to solve the many mysteries of their existence." He emphasized the idea by pointing to his own eyes. "They think that their heavenly home is a single, unchanging reality. Flyers know that heaven is not a location but an expanding thought without limits. The advanced flyers learn to travel inward."

"Inward?" This was a little confusing and he wanted to know more.

"Flyers who can travel inward instead of outward are called navigators. They set their own course and travel within themselves. They don't accept the rules made by the walker flocks. In fact they reject all boundaries and make it their priority to see and explore all the countless inner levels and worlds of heaven. They have no limits. Son, I think you can be a navigator. I am very proud of you."

"Grandpa, I want to be a good flyer!"

"There are many skills to learn. The key is to be open-minded to rapid change within yourself and your surroundings. Realize that nothing is really solid in heaven. All form is created and molded by thought. Even our bodies are created by thought. Let me show you." Billy watched as his grandfather closed his eyes and appeared to concentrate; within seconds his body changed into the shape of a wrinkled old man with thinning white hair and a beard.

Billy was startled by the rapid change as his grandfather explained. "By focusing on the memory of what I looked like before I died and holding it in my mind I can change my outer form to become that image; it's fun! Our focused thoughts shape and mold the outer world of our reality; heaven is made of an amazingly subtle energy and our thoughts can manipulate it. That's how I made this motorcycle," he said as he pointed that way. "Navigators know this and develop their creation skills."

"Grand pop, that's wild! Can I do it?"

"Sure, just focus and hold the image of any person you know; picture them clearly in your mind."

Billy stood up, closed his eyes, and concentrated. Slowly his twelve-year-old body changed into a replica of his best friend from school.

"Excellent! Now just let go of that picture in your mind and you will return to your normal self- image."

Billy quickly converted back to his own recognizable form.

His grandfather glowed with pride. "See what I mean? Our thoughts mold our reality. This applies to everything in heaven. Thoughts shape our entire world. But you have to actively focus and be completely open-minded to immediate change, not just believe."

"How do I travel inward?"

"Think of heaven as a very tall staircase made up of an endless range of levels. As you travel inward each level is a little less dense than the one next to it. The next time you are flying, firmly request to experience the next level within you. Practice saying it: Next Level Now!"

"Next Level Now!" said Billy.

"That's it. Now make this a focused demand and expect an instant reaction. Be completely open to a rapid change in yourself and your surroundings. Stay calm, for your surroundings will begin to dissolve and a new environment will appear. With practice you can travel inward and enter another level of heaven. Each level is within you and is always a part of you. This is controlled flying or traveling inward; there are no limits to how far you can travel within yourself." He hesitated for a moment to see if Billy understood his words.

"We are the living doorway to all the remarkable levels of heaven. They are all within you. With practice you can become an effective navigator in all the levels. No limits! The answers to the big questions of life exist within you. And when you become a skilled traveler of the levels you can begin to guide others to find their way. It's an exciting journey of discovery!"

"Grandpa, that's awesome; but no one believes me."

"Don't give up, one day they will. The Earth-bound walkers will one day understand the importance of flying. Learning the principles of flight is an essential step in our growth. Just have faith in yourself and your abilities."

"I know that it's fun." Billy threw his head back, raised his arms and turned himself around in circles. "Next Level Now!" he shouted to the universe.

"That's right, it is fun," laughed his grandfather. "Just remember, there are no limits to how far or high you can fly. Your only limits are your own thoughts."

"Why can't everyone do this?" Billy stopped and looked at his grand-father, as he intuitively knew that their time together was growing short.

"They all can, but most people are completely focused on their dense outer body. They become comfortable in their material form."

"You mean they limit themselves?"

"Yes. They settle for what they can see instead of searching for the truth." He hesitated then continued. "One day you will teach them to fly and show them how to see beyond the physical." His grandfather went back over to his motorcycle and swung his leg around over the seat.

"No one listens to me, they say I'm dreaming." Billy noticed that the sidecar was no longer there.

"One day they will listen; you will need patience with them. Flying is a big step for people who only know how to walk," he said as he put his hands on the throttle to start up the engine.

"Grandpa, what do I do next?"

"Follow your intuition. Recognize that your choices and experiences will give you the lessons you need. We all learn through our own self-created school of life." His grandfather kicked the starter.

"What can I do to make Mom believe me?" Billy was determined to get in just one more question.

"The next time your mother won't believe you, explain to her that we talked during one of your flights; tell her I have a message for her." He softened his voice and said, "On your mother's wedding day, I reminded her about her dream to become a songwriter. I encouraged her to hold on to that ambition even with the demands of being a wife and mother. Tell her to find the red notebook of lyrics she carried throughout school. She will know what this means."

Billy's grandfather hesitated and said warmly, "Young man, you can do anything you put your mind to. You're amazing! You have no limits; focus and create the life adventure you want." And with that last comment, Billy watched as his grandfather rumbled away from the mountain overlook. "Wahoo!" he yelled with one arm up in the air, waving.

Billy returned to his body with a new sense of purpose. He wrote down what he could remember, and knew his grandfather's thoughts would remain ingrained in his mind forever.

The next morning he could hear his mother's voice echo through the house. "Billy! Breakfast!"

Yes! She made pancakes. "Be right down," he answered.

"How did you sleep last night?" She hesitated to ask.

"Great," he said as he poured syrup over the pancakes on his plate.

"Good. No more dreams, then?"

"Nope. No dreams. But Grandpa says 'hi.' He's got a cool old motorcycle."

"How did you know he rode a motorcycle?" she asked.

"He took me for a ride through the mountains. It was awesome."

"Billy, I . . ."

"I'm supposed to tell you that you shouldn't give up on your dream to become a songwriter. Grandpa said you should find the red notebook you carried throughout school," he said as he put another big bite in his mouth.

The color drained from her face. No one knew about her red note-book. Could it be that Billy really was connecting with another world when he slept at night?

"You haven't been going through my old boxes from the attic, have you?" she grilled her son.

"No, Mom. It was Grand pop, I swear. He's anxious to hear a record-ing of your songs," Billy said.

"Oh, my," his mom said as she pulled up a chair near her son. "I'm sorry I doubted you. Let's talk more about what you've been doing."

"Sure Mom. May I have a few more pancakes first? Flying makes me hungry."

THOUGHT FARMS

I was confident that I was going to have an OBE that night. It was in my affirmations. "I am grateful for the OBE that I am going to have tonight." And then I added: "Hey universe, make it something significant. Not just flying over trees and houses this time."

Placing my head gently on the pillow, I cleared all thoughts of the day from my brain. Over and over I repeated, "I am grateful for the OBE that I am going to have this night." It didn't seem long before I felt the familiar spinning. If you have never had this experience, I can only describe it to you like the scene in the Wizard of Oz where Dorothy has returned to her farm home and is in the middle of a tornado. Her bed rises and spins as the wind becomes stronger. That's what it felt like. I knew I was leaving my body behind so my soul could travel freely. I confirmed it with, "Whee, here I go!" Now, you should understand that I often use this expression to calm any lingering fears that might be left over from when I first began having these exciting adventures. As soon as I say that phrase I know I am in for a safe and fun time.

Anyway, in what seemed like only moments, I found myself in a field. Not like any field that I've ever seen before. I saw that there was dirt under my feet and green stalk-like plants lined up in a row. My first thought was of corn but as I examined the greenery closer, I saw that these were single stems with no fruit. Some were very green and healthy looking, while some were beginning to turn brown, bearing wilted, low-hanging leaves. There was no real consistency to their condition. I walked along the row where I had landed, searching in my mind for the meaning of such an unusual place.

I remembered that asking for help is always an option when out of body, so I shouted, "Is there anyone here who can answer my questions?"

Stepping out of one row was a spritely old fellow. His blue velvet shorts held up by orange suspenders were matched to a blue-and-orange striped, silky shirt. He carried a crooked wand with a light at the tip. Since he was just three feet tall (not counting the pointy red hat that barely covered his ears), I was lucky to have spotted him.

"Welcome. I am Spunk, a curator here." He bowed slightly and smiled. I felt very comfortable in his presence.

"What is this place?" Determining that he was more leprechaun than agricultural engineer, I couldn't make any assumptions about where I was and what I was seeing.

"You have come to *The Thought Farm*," he said as he waved his wand across the area, spreading light with the tip of it so that I could see for miles.

"*Thought Farm*?" This was a new one for me.

"Yes, you see all human minds plant thoughts throughout their life. Some, like this one, are cultivated." Spunk pointed to a nearby stalk. It was bright green and seemed to be growing before my eyes. The soil around the base of the structure was moist and there were some distant musical notes that seemed to be emanating from the center.

"Listen. Such a beautiful melody. Someone in their physical life has selected music to be a part of their legacy." Spunk stopped for a moment to appreciate the lovely sounds.

I felt warm knowing that a human was creating such a delightful atmosphere for their fellow humans to enjoy.

"It was an ambitious thought, but with focus and determination, she made it materialize. One of her goals for this lifetime has been achieved. If she wishes she can fulfill more thoughts or she can be satisfied with her one goal of providing music education in underdeveloped areas that would not otherwise have access to this art form."

"That is a lofty goal. She should be congratulated." I wondered if I had any meaningful thoughts out there.

"We'll get to that." Yikes, can he read my mind?

"Yes. You aren't very good at hiding your contemplations." Spunk began to walk away and I felt compelled to follow him. He moved quickly for such a short-legged guy.

"Because I don't recognize physical constraints," Spunk replied to my subconscious comment. Jeez, I need to be more careful. He stopped for a moment to show me a small shoot.

"This thought was recently planted. It is difficult to know whether it will ever grow or if it even needs to. We call this a starter thought. It might grow tall and healthy, or wither and die, or morph into something else. It is all very dependent on the human mind that has planted it."

"But what if it is something important? And no one cultivates the idea?" I asked.

"That has happened. It is possible that the world is not ready for the outcome. Or that the human mind that created it cannot support the work that is involved. Look at this one now," he said, pointing to a brown, withered stalk. "This one was planted but never given any care or consideration."

That's when I began to think of all of the things I had considered doing as a physical human and how many of those had gone to the bottom of the list as I focused on what I considered as my 'priorities'.

"Again, as I said before we will get to that. First, I have some special ones to share." I was excited about getting the VIP treatment. Spunk just shook his little head and turned toward a white marble door.

"Welcome to *The Thought Museum*. These are some thoughts that were deeply nurtured and made a significant impact on human evolution." The wand went up and the doors slid open. I covered my eyes for a moment as this was an extremely bright room.

He guided me into a covered area that appeared to be the entryway to a display room. The floor was no longer dirt, but a beautiful crystal surface. Instinctively, I removed my shoes so that I could feel the energy coming through my feet.

"My idea." Spunk smiled. He knew I was impressed with the floor and he wanted to let me know that he was more than just a tour guide.

Stalks were lined up against the open-air wall with ample space between them. I was being schooled on thought design. Thoughts need air to breathe. I learned that the more light sent to them, the better their chance for long-term growth. Our energy feeds them, so frequent attention is the best fertilizer.

Along the first row I saw a beautiful, rich-green stalk and under it was a plaque marked *Emancipation*. The next had a plaque that said *Electricity*. We continued and I saw *Crossing the Atlantic* and then *The Acropolis, Birthplace of Democracy*.

"These are in no particular order because the thought is not time-related to the outcome." Spunk looked at me with knowing eyes. "No, you don't see one for the cell phone—we have not decided about that one yet."

He then pointed to a door that had multiple locks. "We will not enter that room. It contains evil thoughts that are cruel and can send the humans to a dark place. There is senseless violence, dishonest behavior, and pain brought on by the thoughts of others. To enter that room would give energy and light to those concepts. And since you have nothing planted there, we shall move on." He sensed my curious hesitation and waved both arms at me. "Quickly!"

As we got back out into the open field, I immediately felt better. But I still needed to see what thoughts I had planted and if there was anything that I needed to fertilize. Maybe I had the cure for a disease in my row of thoughts. Or perhaps I had perfected a new mode of space travel. I was excited for the opportunity to see what I needed to work on.

"Remember, all thoughts are planted here—the incredible and the mundane. And we never know if the mundane will become the incredible. So they are all treated equally when planted."

As we reached our destination, I noticed a small hole where a plant once was. "Yes, our thoughts can be taken from us. If someone wants to put in the effort and you do not, then it can happen. You've heard of the one that got away?"

Our next stop was a stalk about as high as my shoulder. It was pale green and the leaves were just turning a dull yellow.

"Uh-oh." This one did not look too good. I was hoping this was just another example Spunk had for me, not anything that I had planted.

"Well, yes this one is yours."

"What is the thought?" I squeezed my brain to see if I could come up with anything good.

"Only you will know that. I can tell you that it has been around for a while. Every now and then you send it some energy, but you have never really made a commitment to it. Because it is still alive, although barely, there is still a chance for you to make this inspiration a reality."

"But if I don't know what it is, how can I develop it?" I had become motivated to develop this thought into the strong, healthy stalk that I knew it could be.

"You want to ripen this fruit. Your higher self asked to learn something significant during your journey tonight. It doesn't get more crucial than knowing that your thoughts create your reality."

"So what do I do next?"

"An event or message will appear. If you pay attention, you will understand what it is that you want to pursue. Focus on what happens over the next few days. An event, conversation, or meeting will occur that calls for your awareness. This is called your synchronicity key. Take it and it will open the door to your neglected thought."

I sat up in my bed at home and immediately pulled out my journal. I wrote down everything I could remember, and realized that I already missed Spunk. He was inspiring and funny; I wanted him to be proud of me. I vowed to spend the rest of the day focused on my mission. I called it *My Thought Pursuit*. I was driven to find out the plan that I had been neglecting. I listened to meditation music and repeated affirmations. I burned incense, held my crystals, and even swung a pendulum. Not even a hint.

"Honey, don't forget we have dinner plans with the Bakers tonight."

"Arggghh," I thought to myself. "Ok, sounds nice," I replied to my wife.

When we sat down, all that Baker guy wanted to talk about was the vacations that he had taken. Yes, he had cruised through the Panama Canal, climbed a glacier in Alaska, and seen the temples of Angkor Watt. It was less than fascinating to hear about their sightings of the Terra Cotta Warriors in China and the Northern Lights in Iceland. I was starting to zone out when his next comment caught my attention.

"But even traveling all over the world, my absolute favorite vacation was . . ."

It hit me like a ton of bricks—that was the idea that had been sitting neglected for so many years. This was something that I had always wanted to do. There were always excuses: kids to consider, time off from work, money concerns. But now I had the green light and I was going to take it. Perhaps on the surface this was mundane, but as Spunk told me, one never knows where the thought could lead.

––––––

"Long story short . . ."

"My word, way too late for that," thought Miranda, the registration coordinator for Adventure Travel World.

" . . . That is why I am signing up for this trip. I'm turning 60 next month and if I don't do it now, it might be too late." I had my credit card ready and waited for the next bit of information that she would need.

"Well, that is fascinating Mr. Maxwell. And I'm glad to help you with your reservation to raft down the Colorado River in the Grand Canyon. Now, did you say that would be three guests?"

THE FALLING

"Good Mor-ning," he said to me in his usual melodic voice. "Coffee's on, be ready in a few minutes." I could hear him rattling coffee mugs and checking the refrigerator for the half-and-half creamer. I shuffled my purple fuzzy slippers across the hardwood floor and tilted my head up for a sleepy kiss. "Umm, that smells so good." I could tell he had splurged on the good stuff—a local, organic bean that left a satisfying trail of rich mocha scent through the hallway.

My pink nightgown hung loosely over blue-striped pajama bottoms, with a gray sweater over it all. Sounds kind of random, but this was my typical layered outfit that I wore to tame the chilly morning air. My only concession to how I looked was running a comb through my hair when I got out of bed. Somehow it seemed to be enough. After all we had been together for, what . . . thirty five, forty years? Who counted anymore? It didn't seem relevant.

Yes, it was a morning like most others, except this was my last one with him. Or, I imagine, for at least a very long time.

Honoring my morning ritual of playing soft instrumental music, I picked my favorite melody from *Liquid Mind* and plugged it in. Then I pressed the on switch of my computer and placed it to the side. Although we had an unspoken rule about no electronics during our morning coffee talk, I generally turned it on to have it warmed up and ready to go. Why? I don't know. I guess there were a few loose ends that needed to be tied up before the sun reached its peak—the signal that I would soon begin my descent. Finding my divot in the middle section of the couch, I fell back into the multi-colored cushions that served as the backrest to my throne. I stared into the fireplace waiting for my prince to deliver a steaming mug of coffee.

"Here ya go," he said as he did every morning and put the cup on a tray in front of me. I noticed that the tray was a bit scratched and stained where my cup stood as it cooled. "I should have refinished that," I thought, "It's a nice tray but could use a little paint or stain. Or something." There's another thing on my list that won't get done.

He sunk down into his worn leather chair, blowing on and drinking from his cup simultaneously. Oh how I love this man. I look at his face. Sure he's a little older, a little wrinkled maybe, but when I see his eyes they still dance like when we were young. That was always the first thing I saw when I looked at him—those eyes that had so much life in them. I'll miss that. I know I will.

Normally we would have our conversation about our plans for the day, what needed to be done around the house, who we needed to call, what we thought of our neighbor's new driveway—simple things that made us feel like we were accomplishing something. Today was different. The change was unspoken but we both knew it was coming.

"It's been good, right?" I tried to gently approach what I knew needed to be said.

"Sure. I don't think we could have done anything different." Not the romantic reply I was hoping for, but it was a start.

"Remember when we had dinner on the beach in Koh Samui?" I was trying to generate some kind of life review before I left. Yes, before I left. I knew I was going, although truthfully I was trying to delay the inevitable. We had discussed this before, but only now did it seem real.

"Yeah, it was cool to pick out our own lobster from the ice table. The moon was full and bright against the clear, inky sky. I'm so glad we did it. And the weather was just perfect."

"I have to admit, I faced a very real fear on that trip." I slurp some warm coffee.

"Potential food poisoning? High tides?" He shakes his head in agreement.

"No."

"Pirates?"

"Being too full for dessert!" And we laugh. It feels good to laugh.

He gets up and goes into the kitchen for a refill. I stare at the beautiful mountain vista perfectly framed by a huge picture window. We have lived in a few different environments: near the water with a boat dock, in a penthouse apartment in the middle of the city, and raising goats on a country farm. But I think this is my favorite. It's good to end with a pleasant view. It will help me to remember.

"You know, I think this room is nicely put together," he says as he repositions himself in his favorite chair. "I do appreciate all the color—royal-blue velvet chairs, the Asian rug with the red mandala, and the purple wall. Love that wall. I'm so glad we changed the paint so that it stands out against the other boring beige walls," he said with an air of finality that I am beginning to feel from his tone. "We did a good job here."

"I agree. And I love all the books we've collected over the years." I looked toward the massive shelves holding an enormous number of books from internationally recognized authors. "They're colorful on their own, but even more important is that they bring such positive energy into the room." I don't want to add this next point to my vocal comments. Because of the concepts shared in those books, I'm not afraid. It doesn't mean I'm ready, but I think I'm prepared. I hope that 'ready' shows up by the end of the day.

So I know he's not going to bring it up, I know he doesn't want to talk about it. But I must. I cannot go leaving things unsaid. This is so hard to do and delaying is not possible because there is no tomorrow.

"Is there anything I can do for you before I go?" I say, trying to break into the tough topics.

"No, I think I've got everything taken care of." He hesitates and then continues. "You know I've always loved you, right?" It is difficult to look at him. I'm trying to stay so strong, so I glance away toward the mountain. There is a fog developing outside that begins to cast a shadow across the window.

"Yes," is all I can say without choking on the boulder lodged in my throat.

"Do you have a plan?" he asks me.

"Not really; I expect that I will be able to handle whatever happens. I'll probably just wing it."

"If I could change things and go with you, you know that I would." I believe him, but I also know that we have different paths to follow this time.

"I didn't always show it, but I knew we were meant to be together." Did I see him wipe something from his eye? "I will miss you deeply, but I understand your need to go. Who knows? Perhaps we will meet again."

"Are you sorry we never had children?" I ask him, already knowing the answer. I need reassurance that we were in harmony with our decisions.

"I used to think that a family would have been nice, but I would never want them to experience this moment. It's not what I would wish for anyone." He stands, puts his arm on the mantle, and gazes toward the fireplace. I know he is crumbling inside.

I can feel that my session here is rapidly coming to an end. The room is beginning to darken and the colors are fading into various shades of gray. I stand to embrace him, placing my head on his big, firm chest. I can't allow myself to look into those eyes that drew me to him so long ago. The thought that I will not see them again is unbearable.

"You know I've always loved you, too. Even when I didn't." We both smile just a little. I am hesitant to take the next step, but I realize it is no longer in my control. I can feel my arms losing shape, slowly disappearing from my sight. I ask him for confirmation. "My arms are no longer there, are they?"

"No," he says, "they are fading away. And you are losing color, becoming black and white. It must be time." I could always count on him to be honest, to state the truth even when I didn't want to hear it.

"There are voices around me, but I cannot understand what they are saying. Do you hear them?" They are invisible but I think people are dying. Or is it me?

"Good bye, my love," he whispers. "Have a safe journey." I can tell he is looking away from my diminishing form. That is not how he chooses to remember me.

I am not afraid, but I try to squeeze out every last moment. The process has begun and I cannot change the course of my direction at this point. In my thoughts, I wish him peace and comfort in his remaining days.

With reluctant acceptance, I begin to fall slightly back. There is a pressure on my forehead and I am gently pushed into the blackness. As I fall I see my ancestors, hundreds of human forms floating aimlessly through the sky. They are versions of me, shadows of the characters I've been. I am somehow comforted by this gathering, knowing that this is how it is supposed to be. I do regret, though, that I am beginning to lose memory of the man that I just left behind.

I feel that I am camouflaged into the darkness around me. I continue to fall, but ever so gently. Will I be with him again? Inside I know the answer is yes, though when we meet next he will be changed, a different slice of the same pie. I need to reassure myself before I can fully let go.

More voices and they become louder; they are happy, encouraging this event. I remember a chant from a book that I once read. "Higher Self Now! Higher Self Now!" I shout these words because I know that it must be important.

My new landscape is beginning to take shape. People are clapping and laughing. The room is stark but filled with joy. I sense that I have just arrived at my destination. I cry out, loudly. I am not familiar with the language that I am hearing but I feel good vibrations, a high energy level in the atmosphere. Someone lifts me gently and places me in a warm blanket. I feel so much love and appreciation.

I did it! I came back to the physical world. I'm not sure who, but someone in this room needs my help and as I adjust and grow into my new biological body, I must remember why I am here.

CRASH

He was sleeping so soundly that he was unaware that the sun had been bright in the sky for over an hour. David Carlson was consumed with reliving the nightmare that had haunted him since high school.

"Hey guys, get up. Come on, you need to get out of the road before another car comes along."

A sharp pain was building in his throat as he spoke the words. When all was still again, he shook his head and tried to get his mind straight about what had just happened. He smelled the pungent odor of tires burning, heard the hissing steam coming from the engine compartment of the minivan, and saw the smoke twirling eerily by the beam of the only remaining headlight.

There was an unnatural stillness from the passengers who had been thrown from the Jeep. And then through blurred vision, he watched the incredible separation. Each spirit seemed to rise from a broken body and stand next to the tattered remains of what was once young and strong. Rob was one of them; he shook his head as if to wake from a deep sleep. Scott looked around like he'd just been dropped off in an unfamiliar neighborhood. Brenden, the third passenger, just stared in disbelief. David's friends were now in a different world.

"What's happening here?" David turned toward the mini-van. A feminine ghost-like form stepped through the driver's door and looked back into the rear seat compartment at her children. She tried to reach in, to comfort them somehow, but could not.

A pickup truck pulled up behind the mayhem and a man got out offering help, as his wife used her cell phone to make the 911 call. The distant wail of a siren soon broke the gruesome silence. The rescuer went to the van first. When he saw the children and the woman he assumed was their mother at the wheel, he could barely control his own emotion. More people had now stopped to assist as the sound of the siren was getting closer.

From the curbside, David stared at his own unconscious body, which was still belted in the Jeep. Bewildered, he attempted to speak to his friends once more.

"Oh my God, I can't believe it! The Jeep is totaled. My Dad is going to kill me. Are you okay? Come on, one of you say something!" he rambled nervously, hoping his eyes were playing tricks on him.

And then without any sound, a twister of tiny stars moved out of the clear sky down to the scene. It became larger and larger as the walking wounded started gliding toward this beautiful sight. The people who had stopped to help did not sense the change in the air. But David could see every detail.

"Where are you going? Hey, what's happening? Wait!" he called to his friends, and then watched as—one by one—they

began to enter the light beaming down onto the road. One turned toward David and gave a slight nod to him.

"It's so beautiful. Can you see it?"

"Later, Carlson," said another as he, too, glided toward the amazing light show.

The other driver was still standing by her vehicle when a silver cloud settled over the van. The woman was reluctant to follow, as she did not want to leave her children alone in the night. She needn't have worried. When the emergency team arrived, they assessed the scene. The one in charge was giving orders to his subordinates.

"Check the kid in the Jeep." As the EMT touched his wrist, the flash of searing pain drove David's full attention back to his own human form. "Got a pulse. Let's go!" At that moment, David felt his consciousness slam back into the bleeding body, his very own injured and aching body.

Disoriented, he turned his head to look for his friends, but he could only recognize them by their shoes, as now they all had blankets covering their upper bodies. They were barely dead, with still-warm blood pooling around their injuries, their last breaths still lingering in their mouths. Their hopes for the future had not yet left their hearts. He was too shocked to cry out. David was carried to a waiting ambulance, where his gurney was lifted up to the floor of the vehicle.

Alone inside, with the interior lights blinding him, he heard the door slam shut, the siren shattering his stillness.

The sound of his phone ringing finally brought him back to his current life. He felt his arms but could not move them. David tried to get up to answer, but his legs would not follow the command from his brain. The call went to voice mail. David reviewed that night in his head over and over again as if he could somehow affect the outcome.

It happened on a section of the road known as the '*Seven Sisters*,' named for the seven sharp and sometimes deadly curves alternating right and left within yards of each other along the banks of Winterbird Lake. As evidence, several roadside tributes of handmade crosses and faded artificial flowers were planted along the way. Pictures, ragged stuffed animals, and ripped bits of school T-shirts were common sites at these memorials.

Typical for late October, it was cool with a fresh feeling in the air. There were no clouds that night; it was clear enough to see the sharp contrast of each star against the black night sky. On this back country road, there were no streetlights, but the sparse illumination from the mid-evening moon filtering through the stately pines created a mystical reflection on the lake.

They were moving fast, too fast, on the east side of the road in his white classic 80s model Jeep Wrangler. In custom pinstripe, the name "Moby" was stenciled along the back gate; it was named for the classic whale. The convertible top had been removed exposing the teenaged driver and his three friends to the chilly night. Wearing their varsity jackets and matching maroon wool skull caps trying to keep warm in the open vehicle, they were laughing and exchanging friendly insults with each other.

Approaching from the other side was a blue minivan driven by a weary mom, her children singing happily in the back seat. The Jeep began to swerve slightly to the center and for just a moment—a critical moment—he lost sight of the road ahead. Behind the wheel of the minivan, the woman could barely keep her eyes open after a long workday.

What happened next was horrendous. Both drivers saw the oncoming headlights at once, but it was too late to make any significant adjustment in their courses. The crash was inevitable. The Jeep was pounded on the left side of the front fender and flipped side-over-side until it was off the road. The 4 x 4 rolled down the hill, throwing passengers out as it careened toward the shallow, dark lake.

The van went out of control and the force of impact sent the vehicle flying into a massive tree just at the edge of the third sister. The driver hit the windshield with such power that her unbelted upper body was impaled on the steering wheel, and her head made deadly contact with the windshield. Closing his eyes, picturing the scene once again, David tried to analyze what he could have done differently. There must have been something, anything to change the outcome of this horrendous situation.

He heard the screeching of the brakes making a desperate attempt to stop the vehicles, and then the glass of the windows exploding, the crunch of metal on metal, and worse yet, the wretched screams from the passengers in the Jeep. One of those was his own. Confused, David felt his consciousness move out of the Jeep back up to the street where the carnage was still fresh. The children in the back of the van were no longer singing, no longer living. Scared and cold, David recognized his friends. He stood by them, reaching out trying to touch Scott's arm.

But at home, David was alone again in this simple room with nothing to do but think about the wreckage and the horrible days that followed. The accident haunted him still and he wondered—after the hundredth nightmare—if his life would ever be the same. The images of his friends sprawled on the ground were as clear today as if it had just happened. How could he have lived? How could he have been the only one to survive the crash?

Thankfully, David had another appointment to see Dr. Howard. They had met just after he had been put on academic probation at the university. David felt that his instructor could be trusted with his story, and based on his unorthodox research into parapsychology, perhaps even help him. He knew he was fortunate to have such an experienced sounding board. He thought back to the day when they first began to explore his experience.

"Professor Howard, can I talk to you about something personal?"

"Certainly Mr. Carlson, come into my office," Dr. Sam Howard said hoping that he could help to bring some peace of mind to his troubled student. Recognizing the anxious tone in his voice, Sam had ushered him to his private rooms. David had explained the horror of his experience and given substantial detail about the feeling of body-mind separation.

"I was out of my body. I mean I could see my body was somewhere else. I saw my friends. It looked like they went to heaven." Rather than telling him he was crazy, Sam Howard was anxious to hear every detail. He was seeing evidence of post-traumatic stress and after that first session they had become allies in the search for answers.

"Tell me exactly what happened," said Dr. Howard as he began sessions of Cognitive Processing Therapy. If he could get David to see the accident was not his fault, then perhaps he could begin to heal. It was a better option, he thought, than beginning to prescribe medications that only covered the symptoms rather than remove the cause of his distress.

"Like the other kids leaving the football game, me and my buddies were pumped up about the victory over Newark. They were ranked #1, and we were #2. After we beat them, we were tied for state. One more win for us this season and our team would have been headed to a divisional title game. It was our senior year, and going to the Delaware State finals would have meant some scholarships. Scott was being scouted by a few universities. And Brenden could have made it to the one of the Big Ten. He was really smart and probably the best quarterback in the state, maybe the Central Atlantic region."

"So everyone was excited that night. Victory was within your grasp, and football was the most important thing going on in your life. Is that what I'm hearing?" asked the doctor.

"Football and girls. That night we were headed for Tiara Dean's house, where her parents were throwing a big celebration for the team. You know, cheerleader dads could still hang out with the players if they'd throw a party for us."

"Now the game is over and the four of you are headed to a party. Tell me about the driving arrangements." The doctor tapped his pencil to the bottom of his chin.

"It was my turn. We used to take turns so the same guy didn't always pay for gas," David hesitated and then added, "and I insisted on taking the top off the Jeep."

"So it was your turn, but it could just as easily have been one of your friends who was driving. Go on." His therapist was trying to get David to see that it had been a matter of chance that he was behind the wheel.

"It was a cold night, a very cold night. But the weather was dry and the traffic wasn't too bad, so everybody finally agreed to drive with the top down." He stopped for a moment and looked away. "If only I had kept it on, maybe they would still be alive today."

"Okay, everyone agreed, but still you feel guilty. Let's talk about that." Dr. Howard knew this was painful for David, but talking through the trauma was an effective way to smooth out the emotional roller coaster that had been creating so much turmoil in his personal life.

"Of course I feel guilty. I am responsible for the death of my best friends. How would you feel?"

"Not important how I would feel. This is about working through your feelings and getting you to a point where you can get back to living your life. You survived the accident. Denying yourself the opportunity to pursue a meaningful life will not change what happened. I don't believe your friends would want you to waste your life feeling morose and guilty."

"I'm not sure that's possible. It would feel like I had betrayed them to live the kind of life that they would have wanted but was taken from them. I'm sure they would feel that way, too."

"We really can't predict what is happening in their hearts and minds, so I want you to concentrate on what you can do to create some balance in your life. Don't forget to practice the breathing techniques I showed you. We'll talk again next week." With that the doctor stood up and walked David to the door. "And David, you know you can call me anytime if you have the nightmares and want to talk about it."

"Thanks, Doc. Next week, then."

Another episode had occurred and once again he tried to shake it off, but found it impossible.

"Doc, I can't continue living with this guilt. Everybody says that in time, I will get over it, but this is interfering with my life. I've missed classes. I can't develop any relationships because I'm sure they will end abruptly and it will be my fault."

"If you could imagine any scenario that would soothe your guilt, if anything at all was possible, what do you think would help to resolve this open issue with your friends?"

"I don't know. Maybe if I could talk to them, tell them how sorry I am. They were gone so fast, I never had a chance to say goodbye." David stared off into space. "And I lived. There's that part."

"Look, I didn't want to say anything, but there may be a way. It's kind of bizarre . . . I've been doing some additional experiments teaching two of my dream subjects to communicate with the deceased."

"Go on."

"One told me that she actually met her father while in a semi-conscious state. He's been dead for maybe ten years. Now, there's no real evidence or proof, just her word."

"Sam, I need something real, not some . . . dream."

"This isn't a dream, David. It is a conscious meeting with someone on the astral plane."

"Astral plane?"

"Okay, call it heaven if it makes you feel more comfortable."

"And you believe her?"

Sam nodded. "I believe she's telling the truth—at least her perception of it."

David stared at him. "Sam, you know I would do anything to make this right. But I don't know about this. It sounds a little, you know, out there."

"I thought it was worth mentioning, but if you aren't interested, well no harm done." Sam turned toward the door, a little relieved that David wasn't attracted to this option.

"Sam, wait." David looked up at his friend, desperate for something, for some way to see his friends again, to tell them how sorry he was. "You say I can really see them? Talk to them? And it won't be a dream?"

"I'm saying anything is possible, if you believe that it is."

"Alright. I'm in. When can we get started?"

"Come to my office tomorrow at three o'clock. No promises, though." Sam did not want to pursue this avenue, but he had a soft spot in his heart for David. He really believed that seeing his friends just one more time would help him through this and stop the nightmares.

Arriving at the University Psychology Building, David burst through the doors and took the stairs two at a time. He practically skipped down the hall to Dr. Howard's office and laboratory suite. Not bothering to knock, he went through the door like he owned the place.

"How's it going? I'm ready to go. Should I go over to the lab? What equipment should I use?"

"Nice to see you too, David. Now let's slow down and take this one step at a time." Sam had turned to greet him with a handshake and a pat on the upper arm. He was glad to see him approach their experiment with this level of positive energy.

"I want you to know this is a trial, okay? Don't get your hopes up. It might not work." Sam did not want David to hold high expectations. It might bring him down even further.

"But then again, it might," David responded, excited to try anything.

As Sam Howard went into a closed lab room to prepare the equipment, a pale woman appeared in the outer office, entering without a sound. Her torn jeans and grimy white shirt hung loosely on her frail-looking body. Ignoring Sam, she walked straight to David and looked at him through her wet eyelashes. Tears never fell, but the image on her face was of great sadness.

"Hello. I'm David. Are you part of this experiment?" David asked the woman who had joined them. In spite of her unprofessional appearance, he reached out his hand to shake hers.

"Name's Lexi," she replied without extending her own hand in return. "I'm glad you're here. I understand you are struggling with an event from your past?" Lexi asked him with a quiet curiosity.

"Yeah, but it's kind of personal. Dr. Howard suggested this exercise, needed to try something new." David was surprised to see that Sam had chosen this student as a lab tech. Her social skills were a bit weak.

"We can get started in a moment. Just a few more adjustments and we'll be ready to go." Sam was energized flipping switches and recording data in one of his many notebooks.

"Let's get some privacy for a minute." Lexi led David out to the hallway. Sam stayed busy in the lab, while David listened to what she had to say.

"Why the sudden interest in astral travel? For real," asked Lexi. She stared at David, judging his words carefully.

"Astral?"

"Yes, if you are separating your consciousness from your body. That's what it's called. You've probably heard the term before—an out-of-body experience." She looked impatient.

"I would like to meet and talk to my high school friends one more time. Do you think it's possible, through this astral travel you're talking about?" explained David.

"Anything is possible if you're motivated."

"I am. Motivated is an understatement. I'm driven beyond words." David had never meant anything so sincerely.

"You seem to have forgotten that you have done this before," Lexi reminded him.

"I don't understand."

"When the accident happened, you told Dr. Howard that you were able to see your friends as they left your world," she said as she tucked a lock of stringy hair behind her ear.

"I did. I saw them and I was fully aware that my body was in a different place, but I didn't feel like it was a part of me." David wondered how she knew this. Wasn't there some kind of confidentiality thing between the doctor and him?

"That was a spontaneous event. It can be different when you self-initiate. Some think it's intense, occasionally even frightening," she continued, knowing she had to watch her words more carefully.

"I can handle it."

Lexi hesitated before she spoke again. "Yes, I think you can. But if it does get rough, remember that you are always in control, nothing can harm you. Anything that is uncomfortable or unwelcome is something that you created. You have to embrace it before you can continue your travels."

"I'll do it. For the sake of my friends, I'll face anything that comes my way." Lexi smiled at his response and directed him to the bed in the chamber. She couldn't believe how easy this was going to be. After so many years of waiting, he was finally here. And if she could make this work, she would be free, free to move on with her own journey.

"Good, David. You've found the meditation bed. Now just lie down and I'll be in to fasten your BSD," Sam directed David.

"My what?"

"Brain Synchronization Device." Sam couldn't help but be excited about having a new subject and more documentation of his findings.

"Remember to maintain your focus away from your physical body at all times. The instant you think about your arms or legs or hands, you will snap back into it and the experience is over." Sam gave some last-minute instructions as he adjusted some wire connections.

Lexi leaned forward, confiding in him. "Don't worry, you're a natural. Your desire will propel you forward, not that 'device' he insists on using. Just focus on where you want to be and your consciousness will take you there."

"So, basically, we go where our thoughts lead us."

"Yes, that's right, David. You know more about this than you think," said Lexi.

Sam approached him with a notebook in one hand and a tape recorder in his hand. He began to give directions.

"It's time. It's important for you to have as few distractions as possible. That's why it's just the two of us today. I will lead you through the exercise, and take help as we need it."

"But, what about . . ." David couldn't get his question about Lexi out before Sam began to move on.

"Close your eyes and take several deep breaths. Completely relax. Follow what I say. David I want you to picture your friends as clearly as you can," and with these words, Sam started to lead the instruction.

David took several deep breaths and became increasingly relaxed, forgetting about the woman in the next room.

"Now, repeat the affirmations. Remember to make them your last conscious thought as you drift off."

David nodded his head in agreement.

"I remain aware as my body goes to sleep," Lexi chanted in her now-husky voice.

"I remain aware as my body goes to sleep," followed David.

"Now, I separate . . ."

"Now, I separate . . ."

An intense buzzing sound filled the air as his ethereal form slowly moved up, lifting his perception of a physical body. His eyelids were fluttering with rapid eye movements as his ghost-like upper body sat up, but he struggled to separate from the sleeping duplicate. In frustration, he rocked his energy form in an effort to break free. After several attempts, he rolled sideways and found himself fully upright. In that moment, as he stood next to his physical body, the universe was a swirling chaos of energy. He was disoriented, but recognized the precursor to a controlled dream.

"I want to be aware," David said to no one in particular. "I want to see my friends again."

He stepped away from his body and reached his hand out to touch the interior fixtures in the lab. A coarse vibration sound emanated as his hand entered the block wall. Closing his eyes, he took a step and passed through the structure. Spinning surges of energy flashed by as he moved through each level. He reappeared at the exterior of the building and stared with wonder at his new surroundings.

"I can fly!" David just thought it and he spread his arms and launched himself like a bird. He swooped down the side of the structure and glided several feet above the ground, then moved his arms back and landed perfectly on his feet. Instantly, he rocketed straight up to almost one hundred feet. Flailing his arms awkwardly, his body rolled and dipped, but he eventually gained control over his flight and leveled off. That's when a swirling vortex of shimmering astral light appeared, giving rise to a lush green field extending as far as he could see. One by one, white lines appeared every ten yards. Cheering crowds had filled hundreds of rows of seats and flags were waving. He could hear a marching band and then . . .

The stadium was full of cheering fans that night. David stood in the players' tunnel watching as the clock ticked down and the crowd counted with it. 4,3,2,1 and BUZZZZ. The game had ended and the players in the maroon-and-gold colors were jumping on each other, shouting and rushing around with their arms in the air. Their victory fueled this joyous celebration.

They began to run off the field toward him and soon David was surrounded by sweating and dirty—but jubilant—players as they made their way to the locker room. A couple of the guys acknowledged David with a high five or nod as they rushed past him. He was swept up in the movement and found himself in the victors' locker room.

He stood by the door, not sure whether he was welcome during this celebration. As the players began to shower and change to their casual clothes, David was recognizing a few faces. Scott was towel-slapping Brenden, creating wet streaks on his khakis. Rob was clearing steam from a mirror so he could comb his hair.

"Hey Rob. Who are you getting all beautiful for?" Scott teased his friend.

"I thought I might get to know Jessica a little bit better tonight. You know, winning touchdown and all," Rob shot back, knowing that Scott had always had a thing for her.

"Why, you . . ."

Brenden held Scott back from his mock swing at Rob. Nothing would go wrong tonight. First the state champs and then to a victory party. This really was heaven.

"David, come with us?" Brenden asked his friend at the door.

Before David could respond, he found himself at an upper-middle-class house near the beach in Lewes. A local band was playing in the background as he approached a table with drinks. He selected a clear icy beverage and drank with total pleasure as though he hadn't had a drink in days. Scott approached him. He didn't say a word, just showed him his new ring with the gold championship logo, a solitary red stone in the center.

Brenden came over and tapped his shoulder and spoke to him.

"David. Dude. It's cool. We're okay."

"Yeah. We've never had such a winning record," added Scott.

"Is that really Rob over there holding hands with that hot girl?" asked David.

"Yeah, he thinks he's in love," said Brenden as he rolled his eyes and looked back at Scott.

"You all look like you're having a blast," said David.

"It's not bad. Lucky we all came over together. We've created a pretty good life here." Scott put his hand on David's arm as reassurance.

"Yeah, man. Go home. This isn't for you. You know where to find us when it's your time," added Brenden.

David woke up with a shudder and forced himself to reactivate his legs and arms so he could swing over to the side and hop off of the bed. Sam was standing nearby with pen in hand.

"Well? Tell me what happened," he said anxiously.

"They were all there—Scott, Brenden and Rob. First, we were at the football stadium after a big win, and then they took me to a party." David shook his head in disbelief. "How could they all be so happy? They didn't even act like they were dead."

"I'm not sure but I've heard that there are small social groups that have crossed and continue to be friends and neighbors. Maybe they are part of one those groups."

"Thanks, Dr. Howard. I think I need to go home now and process what just happened."

"Great. This is the most extensive experience we've had here in the lab. Make sure you write down all the details, everything that you can remember: colors, sounds—everything!"

At home, David did just that. Five pages in his notebook were filled with all the elements he had observed. He wrote down their conversations, what they were wearing, and even the background noise. At the end of the journaling, he felt like he had the closure he was looking for. His friends were clearly not suffering, had no regrets, and certainly were not placing any blame on him. The mountain of guilt that he had been carrying for years had been lessened. Could it be that he had been harboring these feelings with no justification? The only lingering doubts were about those children in the van. He never did find out what happened to them.

He was exhausted now. He sank back into his sofa cushions for just a minute to rest his eyes.

David found himself walking down the road where the accident had occurred. All was quiet; he felt like there was just one open issue that still needed resolution. As he turned the corner, he felt a slight pressure in his chest when he saw the maimed tree. It deepened when Lexi unexpectedly appeared standing next to it.

"Hello there. Don't I know you from Dr. Howard's lab?" David asked, already knowing the answer.

"Yes, that's where we did our work," she answered softly.

"Our work?"

"You were not the only one with unfinished business after the accident." She let it sink in for a moment. "I was driving the van. I carried every bit as much guilt as you did."

"But why?"

"I fell asleep at the wheel, wasn't wearing my seat belt. Shouldn't have been driving my little babies like that," she admitted to him and looked away. "So you can imagine my shame. Not only did I have a part in transferring your friends, I sent my children to the other side without their mother." She folded her arms and glanced toward the spot where her van had crashed.

"So why did you appear to me in the lab?"

"Because the only way for me to move on was to help you heal. There were consequences for my behavior. I've been stuck here at this sight waiting for a way to connect with you,

a way that wouldn't scare you. I knew you trusted Dr. Howard, so I helped a little bit with his experiment."

"He didn't know you were there?" David asked.

"Of course not. He's a scientist."

"Then I have to thank you," said David. "Seeing my friends, knowing that they're okay is a priceless gift. Words cannot express to you how much better I feel. I think I can finally move on to a better place in my life."

"That's what I needed to hear," she said. A beautiful beam of light came down to where she stood. David had seen this twister of stars before. A glow of pure love surrounded her as she smiled and looked up. He followed her gaze and felt the peaceful sensation that encircled her gradually fading form. "Oh, do you see them? They're waiting for me." She raised her arms and began her ascent as she became one with the light beam.

There was a single flickering lamp lit when David awoke in the night. He looked at the crystal-patterned shadows dancing across the wall, knowing that Lexi had been reunited with her children. He stood at the window and opened the curtains to a wide-open view. Beyond that window was the rest of his life and he was anxious to get it started.

SOUL SISTERS

There were hundreds of tables in the banquet hall; some were round with six or eight people chatting and warmly greeting each other, others were long and rectangular, seating as many as twelve. Positioned around the interior, there were even a few tables for two or four that were scenes of some intense conversations. This was *The Wheel*, a primary meeting and planning center for one of countless soul communities on the astral level.

Whether they were looking over menus, toasting their reunion, or laughing about shared past experiences, it was clear that the members of this soul community had known each other for many lifetimes. While some were reconnecting in the festive atmosphere, others sat waiting silently for their soul mates to arrive.

Earth-tour counselors wearing white jackets scurried between tables, notepads in hand, ready to help process the next journey for each partici-pant. Earlier, when Kiran checked his table plan, he was happy to see that Tina and Maris would be at *The Wheel* later in the day. They were a fun pair who always seemed to be up for an adventure. He had led them through many life experiences. And many bottles of Astral Vineyards Wine.

"Hey, Maris! I'm over here." Tina waved to her friend as the hostess led her to the small table by the window. Tina purposely sat at the table facing the door so she could catch Maris as she entered the hall. It seemed like it had been a lifetime since they had seen each other and she was anxious to catch up. She had already waved to Kiran, their personal counselor (and sommelier, if the truth be known), and requested a glass of chilled Chardonnay for each of them so they could begin their chat right away.

"It's been so long since we've talked. I can't believe you went to the earth world without telling me. I thought I'd totally lost contact with you. Sit down and tell me everything," said Tina as she gave her friend a warm hug.

"First, I have to say, Tina, you look amazing. I can tell it's been good for you to stay here, to be grounded for a while," said Maris as she fell back into her cushioned chair and curled both hands around the stem of her wine glass. "Anyway, I'm sorry I didn't bring you on this one, but it was something I had to do on my own. Thankfully, I wasn't gone that long."

"Well, what happened?" Tina took a sip and eyed up her friend.

"I had an agreement with someone I met in the elevator. They were desperate and couldn't find someone to help them, so I went in as a volunteer. I must admit, it was one of the roughest assignments I've ever taken." Maris paused as she reflected on her recent travels. Tina encouraged her to continue. "I incarnated as a baby, a baby who wasn't going to be physical for longer than a few days. I did it to help the family. Don't ask me how or why, but that was the mission. I'll leave it to the ones who agreed to be the family members to work through it." Maris stared across the room as she sipped from the glass in front of her. "It was a really sad situation, I'm so glad for it to be over. Anyway, I want something fun this time."

"Or how about true love?" Tina was a perpetual romantic and seemed to blossom whenever the subject of love came up.

"Yeah like when we were part of the construction crew that was building the Panama Canal." Maris reflected on their life together then. It was difficult being poor in Panama, but they had each other. She had played the role of Luis, the love-struck neighbor who had loved Isabella since they were children.

"No matter how hard you were working, you always managed to stop what you were doing and smile. I remember sometimes you would bring me a pretty rock that had been in the pile. To me, it was like getting the rarest gem in the world." Tina smiled at the memory of her character, Isabella.

"You were beautiful. I wanted you to notice me." Maris looked at her friend with fond memories.

"Well, I did. And so did my brother who worked alongside you," Tina reminded her.

"I'll admit it took me some time to convince him that I could provide a good life for you. But when I got your family's blessing I couldn't have been happier." Maris lifted her glass to toast Tina.

"We did have some good years," Tina admitted.

"Not nearly enough. When that wall collapsed, it was the end of my world," said Maris with a wistful look in her eyes.

"But I was so proud of you. After the kitchen was destroyed and all of us were sent back here, you stuck around and remained strong for my family. They really needed that from you. In everyone's heart you were always Isabella's husband. If they couldn't have me, at least they had Luis and little Mia."

"She looked so much like you—her eyes, her smile." Maris remembered the little girl fondly.

"Of course she did—but it was really Lorinda. She knew what was going to happen and wanted to make sure you had someone from your team there to support you." Tina confirmed what Maris already knew.

"Where is Lorinda anyway? I thought she was going to meet us here for lunch." Maris started looking around the meeting room.

"She might be at the buffet already. All that food reminds me of when we went on that cruise together."

"I know how much you liked the food service when we were on that cruise, but Lorinda says she will never get on a ship again, no matter what life she slides into. That last ship we were on sank like the Titanic."

"Again, I have to remind you, it WAS the Titanic!" Tina tapped her finger against the table.

"Yeah, that's one physical life experience I guess I'm trying to for-get. How about Chinese food?" Maris pointed to the menu.

"Let's not go back to Asia—I did not appreciate working in those rice paddies; I thought I would break my back stooped over all day, every day. You got to be the boss, so it didn't have the same impact for you. Next time it's my turn to have the fun job," said Tina.

"Is that Oliver over there? Look away! Don't make eye contact! He always wants to go with us. He is so afraid of everything—you know it slows us down when we have to watch out for him. He carries everything with him. I don't know how he survives at all." Maris turned her chair.

"I know. One time your parachute doesn't open and you're afraid of heights forever!"

"Right? He is even afraid of the water since the transatlantic ship inci-dent. He needs to learn to stop carrying fears from life to life," said Maris.

"Well, I don't want to teach him," Tina admitted as she tossed back the last of her wine.

"You can't, even if you wanted to, ladies. You know he has to learn on his own." Kiran, their order guide, stood listening to their conversation. "Remember how much fun you two were having in the 1920s?"

"Yes, it was wonderful—glitzy parties, expensive dinners, fine clothes. The stock market crash ended our little adventure too soon. As a couple we didn't think we could make it in poverty so we jumped from that window when all was lost. I suppose we should've stuck around, but I just couldn't bear the thought of constant struggle."

"You didn't learn the whole poverty thing, so you had to come back as poor laborers working on that canal." Kiran was trying to remind them about lessons when he was interrupted.

"Lorinda! There you are. We were wondering if you were going to join us in our next life." Tina was happy to change the subject. No one wants to hear about lessons—that's the hard stuff.

"That's why I'm here." She sat down with her team and Kiran instantly brought her a glass of wine.

"Thanks, sweetie, this is just what I need right now." Lorinda chugged her drink and with astral efficiency Kiran refilled her glass and discreetly floated away.

"So where have you been? We missed you at the last planning summit. We had to leave without you." Maris placed her hand on Lorinda's clenched fist.

"You wouldn't believe it. Remember when I said I wanted to be in a fit, sexy body? And that I wanted to travel, see new places, and have someone special adore me?" Lorinda scooted her chair closer to the table.

"Sure, that sounded like an easy one. How was it?" asked Tina.

"It was a freak show!" Her eyes bugged out while she sipped her wine, making the girls laugh. Lorinda always did have a flair for the dramatic.

"It couldn't have been that bad. Give us the scoop," urged Maris.

"Seriously, ladies. It actually was a freak show. In a traveling carnival. I was a contortionist. Pretty hot, I might add—but that turned out to be a curse."

The friends leaned in. "Details. We want details."

"Every week we traveled to a new town." Lorinda waved at Kiran for another refill.

"Interesting. Go on." Without even looking up, Tina lifted her empty glass too so he would be sure to bring back enough wine for them all.

"You would think so, but every place started to look alike. In the summer, we stayed in all the dusty, hot towns across the midwest USA. In the winter, we hit all the dusty, hot towns across the southwest USA. Even the people looked the same. Kids laughed at us, women screamed, and men shifted in their seats, trying to look tough or worse—bored." Lorinda rolled her eyes.

"Sounds brutal," said Maris.

"It was. We lived in our trailers. There was no time to see anything because we always arrived just in time to hang posters and set up the folding chairs. With sketchy plumbing, long hours, and the same lousy slop for food. Every. Single. Day." She pounded her fist on the table three times to emphasize the point. "Not to mention the constant fighting between the gamers and the ride jockeys," she continued.

"Doesn't sound like that's what you signed up for." Maris thought it was funny, but tried to keep a straight face.

"Well, I wanted to travel. Check. I wanted a strong, fit body. Check. I wanted to be adored. Check."

"Well at least there is that," said Tina.

"Sure. The guy in our troupe that had an elephant trunk for a face wanted to sweep me off my feet. And I could always count on at least one letch in the audience who wanted to see me bend over to entertain him in the front row. Even the bearded lady was a little in love with me. Thank God for that strep infection or I'd still be there." Lorinda gulped her wine.

"Harsh," Tina and Maris said simultaneously.

"Sounds nasty," added Tina.

"Yup. That's the last time I'm going to ask for a self-centered life. I'm beginning to think we might want to listen to Kiran when he tries to help with our choices. That menu selection was too focused on me and not enough on others. That seems to be a theme in my lives. You never know how the lessons are going to manifest. Anyway, I'm going to pass on the next trip. I need some time to rest and reflect . . . and take a hot shower!" She got up and grabbed her purse. "Best of luck to you guys. I'll see you when you get back and you can tell me all about it."

"Bye Lorinda!" they said in unison.

Thinking about Lorinda's recent experience, Tina turned to Maris and said, "Maybe I'm ready for a quiet life on a farm. We could raise chickens and goats, grow our own food."

"Sounds a little boring," Maris said, shaking her head in disagreement.

"We could develop sustainable products and teach the community about working with the Earth planet instead of poisoning it." Tina was trying to convince her friend.

"Hmm. That's a possibility," said Maris, but she wasn't really interested in getting her hands dirty again. "Did you check the specials? Maybe there's something we haven't thought of. Where's Kiran?" She waved to their counselor. "Are there any new items on the menu that we should know about?"

"Yes—we have a young African-safari tour guide who is kidnapped by poachers and held for ransom in order to free one of their gang mates from prison. It's a sacrifice role if you need one."

"I don't think that will end well. Maybe we should tell Oliver about that one. He needs something to help with his fear issues," said Tina. Maris giggled and tapped Tina's glass to acknowledge the suggestion.

"Ok, well, there is a mediocre actress in Spain trying to raise her daughter on her own while working on her career and developing the skills to balance both priorities," Kiran offered.

"No—we want to go at the same time. Mother-daughter options are out." Tina provided this as an additional condition.

"Well, then, you could have the twin package. Both of you are similar with compatible intelligence, but one will end up as a world-famous scientist and the other will be a housekeeper. It is not predestined—so there could be some surprises with that one. This is a lesson on defining success."

"I've always wanted to dance. Do you have anything where I could dance?" Maris was waving her arms in a flowing motion across the table.

"Let me check with the chief guide on duty; would you like another glass of wine while I review the possibilities?"

"Awww, Kiran, you know us so well."

In a soft flash, Kiran moved from their table over to a semi-circular desk in the corner. It was divided into multiple sections with rotating screen shots of different souls in their current life situations. There were books, loose pages and small notes on the surface, and all were masterfully manipulated by the chief guide on the shift. Located inconspicuously in the back of the room, it was where the counselors went to review universal life selections that were available.

"I have a soul looking for a life in dance," said Kiran.

"Half the souls out there want to dance," said Blue, the chief who was covering this shift. A green light flashed from below the desk indicating that a soul had accepted its next incarnation and was leaving the hall. All business, he made a note in his ledger.

"Yes that's true, but I think Maris would actually be good at it." Kiran was trying his best to garner a good assignment for two of his favorite souls.

"Sure, okay. Let me see what's available," he said not even looking up from his station. "Here's one," Blue offered as he swiped his hand over an electronic screen. "In Bangkok she would have an opportunity to entertain others through dance, but not like she imagines."

"Is there something for her companion?" Kiran knew that question would come up.

"Does she like monkeys?"

"Doubtful."

"Well the dancing slots are generally filled very quickly, but I do have an ice skating position open."

"That might work." Kiran was hopeful.

"But she will be injured during her peak performance days and will have to effectively change both her thinking and her vocation," said Blue as he ran his forefinger along the new life register.

"Don't tell me—her companion is the one who attacks her."

"Yes, that's correct—but whatever you do, don't tell her. They will know each other only as fellow competitors. There should be no known animosity or the connection won't work," said Blue. He used the eraser end of his pencil to flip through some additional pages that had just been made available to him.

"Hmmm," he murmured as he landed on a highlighted line item. Tapping the page, he said, "Don't forget we have Archai, a new soul that we need to place with a team that can handle some unpredictable activity. He has been waiting for some time now." Blue had been trying to place Archai, but most experienced souls were reluctant to add a new player to their soul group.

Kiran remembered his first meeting with Archai. As a new soul he needed to be taught how the system worked. "In this wheel," Kiran waved his arms across the expanse of the circular room, "is the incarnation community. There are so many communities that no one has ever attempted to count them. So for now, we'll just focus on this one. These are the many souls that travel in similar embodiment plots. Sometimes they end up in the same experience, depending on what they would like to learn, and if we think it is appropriate, we will coordinate members from different teams."

"So, they will all slide to the physical world together?" asked Archai.

"Not always. Sometimes there is an overlap in life experiences—such as war or a large-scale natural disaster—and some may never be in the same physical script with all of the others."

"Then what is the purpose of the soul group?"

"The soul group is a smaller team that interacts more frequently, but not exclusively. It is the preference of many souls to travel with those whom they can trust."

"And what is this concept of soul mates?"

"This is a term that has been romanticized on the earth planet. It is actually a spiritual partnership that transcends physical and even emotional connections. When in human form, souls can sometimes spend precious time searching for their soul mate as a lover, when it could be anyone who has a special place in their life."

"Such as . . . ?"

"Soul mates could be siblings, co-workers, neighbors, or friends. It all depends on the plan they created before they left the community."

"How do they find each other on that planet with such a massive population?" asked Archai.

"It isn't so important that they recognize the label, but that they live up to the arrangement that they developed together. The mates almost always travel together; they may want to relive the good times that they shared or even make amends for the more unpleasant ones. Members of their team play a support role and souls in the community may or may not be a part of the life they have created."

"Sounds confusing, but I'm ready to join in the adventure!" Archai was excited to be in the community and looked forward to being part of a team. Someday with enough experience, he knew he would be someone's soul mate.

Kiran's attention was drawn back to the current conversation, knowing that inserting Archai into someone else's journey could be good for all involved.

"I forgot about Archai. That might be perfect for them. They could use some coaching experience. I'll see if I can fit that into their next slide. I'll go back and see if any of those options appeal to them."

"Hey Kiran! Over here. I think we've decided," Tina told him.

"We want to be normal, average, suburban parents," Maris added.

"Boring, safe, uneventful life," Tina stressed to Kiran.

"Perfect," he thought. "That should be easy enough. I can get you into a nice home, good friends, fulfilling careers, and healthy lifestyles."

"What's the catch?" Tina looked over at Maris and gave her a look that indicated her suspicions.

"No catch. You'll have a daughter and perhaps more." Kiran thought to himself, if the lead agent wants to add some extra drama to their situation, he'll place Oliver with them also. Kiran decided to make that suggestion. It might be just what Oliver needs to face some fears.

"Should be a nice easy situation, but first I would like to introduce you to Archai." A young, excited participant joined them at their table.

Their next incarnation ….

As teenagers, Tim (Tina) and Mary (Maris) met each other at a high school sporting event and instantly connected on a romantic level. They eventually married and began a simple but contented life together. After some time, as planned, they became parents of two very different children. Their daughter Olivia (Oliver) was born first. She was especially timid, a quiet girl who kept to herself. Olivia needed the night light switched on every evening and would rarely venture to the backyard without one of her parents around. At age six, she was introduced to the school system. She cried a little when she was taken to school on to the bus as she was always concerned about crashes.

Soon she was greeted by a little brother. Archie (Archai) was full of energy and curious about everything. He wanted to touch, smell, or taste everything in his reach. When he became part of the family, Olivia turned out to be very protective, trying to keep her sibling away from the dangers she knew lurked around every corner. One day when he was not even four years old, the family was in the yard preparing a barbeque lunch party for friends. Tim and Mary were busy hanging some string lights on the patio when Archie began chasing a ball. It had picked up motion from the wind and kept rolling toward their backyard swimming pool. Olivia was playing with her dollhouse under the big oak tree, but something told her to turn and watch her brother. Before she even heard the splash, Olivia knew what was about to happen. She jumped up and ran toward him as he followed the ball into the deep end of the pool. Even as her fears were overwhelming her, she did not hesitate to leap into the six feet of water to save her baby brother. Love for another had outweighed her fear.

As a result of this nearly fatal accident, Tim and Mary signed their children up for swimming lessons and they both excelled. Eventually Archie became a lifeguard on Virginia Beach and volunteered as a swimming coach at the Boys and Girls Club. Many years later, Olivia used her new-found bravery to become a travel photographer. She toured internationally, placing herself in dangerous situations to document natural beauty all over the world.

When they were comfortable that both Archie and Olivia had grown into responsible adulthood, Tim and Mary knew it was time for them to return home.

"Well, Mom and Dad, how was your last life?" Kiran asked as he presented a new vintage of Astral Vineyards Cabernet Sauvignon.

"You tricked us. That was Oliver wasn't it?" Tina asked. "I don't see him here. Did he stay a little longer?"

"He hasn't come back yet, but we expect him soon," Kiran assured them.

"That Archai is a little bit of a challenge," Maris added. "We almost lost him early on. Not a good indication of how we were as parents."

"Olivia, I mean Oliver, needed the opportunity to overcome fear. Archie gave her that chance. If you had interfered, the lesson would be lost and everyone would have to start again." Kiran seemed to have all the answers.

"Well, let us know when Oliver comes back so we can meet him at the gate. Just to make sure he has some company."

"How very thoughtful of you," Kiran said as he placed the bottle on their table. He spotted Archai across the room, where he was waving enthusiastically in their direction. Tina and Maris waved back and Kiran nodded that he would be there in a moment. Perhaps Archai had finally found his soul group.

"He was our daughter after all." And with that Tina and Maris toasted to Oliver's role in their last life with a sip of that new red that Kiran had given them.

BLOCK OF ICE

My eyelids are pried open, exposing my eyes to a blast of white-hot light. The burning glare moves from side to side, easing up only to return, piercing my sight again and again. There is a pounding tension on my forehead pushing me into the padded surface behind me. It is unbearable. I cannot move my head to relieve the pressure. Or any part of my body, I realize, as I try to stop this painful process. What is holding me down?

Only when my eyes are forced open can I see. For this brief moment, I realize that I am in a bed surrounded by tubes and lines of liquid dripping into my body. And more sections of hose hanging from the bedside seem to be collecting my output. There are machines above and around my head. I hear a steady whirr, and then a metered whoosh, whoosh, whoosh behind me. Accompanying these is a staccato beep, hum, beep, at my side. The rhythm continues. Beep, hum, beep—pause and then again, beep, hum, beep. Where am I? Have I become part of some magnificent mechanical structure? Am I the hero or villain in this science fiction movie?

Through a haze of fog I see the blurred outline of a man in a lab coat. He blends into another man, perhaps someone with him taking notes. Then blackness surrounds me as they move away. I strain to hear the subtle echoes from the far side of the room. The voices sound as though they are coming through a tunnel, a slow and drawn-out moaning. After a moment,

I feel the ricochets of that same moaning, followed by complex, foreign words that I cannot understand.

Just as quickly, I am once again alone. I try to move my legs but I feel as though I am trapped in a large block of ice. Crushing force from all sides keeps me in this immobile state. As active physical existence becomes a fleeting memory, my head begins to float above me, seemingly detached from my frozen body.

Where am I? I try to gather my thoughts as they seem to have scattered all over this room. My last memory is the noise—a continuous squeal of rubber challenging the concrete road. I'm punching the brakes, turning into the spin, my foot slamming into the pedal again and again. I feel the crunch of metal as I am being slammed into a wall, my car crumpling around me in slow motion. There was a voice. What did it say? "We're with you. You are safe." First the audible caress of those sweet, angelic tones, then the scream of a siren in the distance and finally—total darkness.

I cannot move at all. The pain in my legs is unrelenting; I cannot do anything to massage the tightness I feel there. I am not hungry and yet there is an enormous emptiness inside me that I fear will never be filled.

Someone approaches. It is a woman. She takes my hand and gently squeezes it. "We love you so much. Please come back to us." I cannot respond, but in my head I am thinking, "Have I gone somewhere? Where do I come back from?" She challenges me. "Just squeeze my hand if you can hear me."

I can hear her so I try to respond by moving my fingers. It seems to be working, but she only cries. Did I do it? Did I do what she asked? She sobs and falls into a chair near me. I can't see her anymore but I feel her presence. She is so sad. I have disappointed her. Someone else enters our space, invading our private moment. He is speaking to her now.

"He's fit for his age. That's a plus. We'll know more in the next 24 hours. But I have to be honest. His injuries are severe. If he does make it, there is no way to know how much he will be able to function. He will not likely be mobile—not the man you once knew." There is more crying now. I feel so bad that I cannot make her feel better. In my head I'm shouting, "Please don't cry. I'm trying as hard as I can!"

She kisses my forehead and tells me she loves me before she is gone again. I can't remember her name, but I feel like I know her.

Lightness and darkness weave through the room, sometimes with sounds, other times nothing. I hear the term 'life support' but nothing about this is supporting my life. I was a marathon runner with a penthouse apartment overlooking Lake Michigan, about to be a grandfather for the first time. I was vice president of the company where I worked. I remember an Italian sports car and plans for a safari vacation in the Serengeti. These devices are not taking me back to that life. This line of thinking exhausts me.

Although I continue to try some kind of movement, my muscles are still refusing my commands. My eyes remain closed, although I try so hard to open them on my own. As though I am performing an inventory of my senses, I check the others. Smell seems to be intact but there is nothing familiar here, only antiseptic and something burning. I try to imagine a tray of freshly baked cookies in place of the rancid odor of flesh and bones that no longer serve their master. If I am touching anything, I would not know as I have lost most of the feeling in my fingers. There is nothing to taste as my tongue sticks to the roof of my mouth. Occasionally someone will swipe a wet sponge across my lips, but a metallic sensation remains.

Time goes by—hours, days? Hot bolts of pain shoot down my right side and sadly I am still unable to move any part of my body. I feel the incoming burn of liquids as they are continuously being pumped into my system. It reminds me of filling my car at the gas station and I wonder if this is the fuel that keeps my brain from relaxing. As I become more aware in my current state of being, it is clear that the whoosh I hear is actually in sync with my breathing. Is this how I operate now? In total stasis—every function is an artificial movement?

A man speaks again. "This is likely a long-term condition. I don't think there is any hope for recovery beyond this point. The medical term is 'consistent vegetative state.' " Regrettably, my hearing remains sharp.

The mood of the room sinks lower than I thought was possible. I welcome the comfort of blackness and as it engulfs me, I can feel something different. It is a subtle shift in energy that sends me spinning inside of my body. It is not physical, but it is soothing. I begin to hear familiar voices. They want to help me. I feel love and support. My eyes open and as I adjust to the low lights I can tell they are holding me, helping me to walk. My legs are unsteady but I am moving. Am I dreaming?

It is so peaceful and warm as I listen to soft piano music. I feel like I have come home. My body has returned control to my mind and it is comfortable and free. There is kindness here—love and caring. I feel like I can release the weight of this physical body.

Ahhh, no! The eyelids, again. Fingers are pulling at my eyelids, the hot lights blasting away my paradise. Leave me alone, I try to say.

It's her again, taking my hand. She is reading poetry to me in a trembling voice. Occasionally she stops and I hear her take deep, measured breaths. I wonder as she takes a pause if she is expecting me to respond. As hard as I try, there is nothing I can do to make her smile again. Somehow I know she holds the key that will set me free from this prison. Will she help me to melt this ice and let my spirit soar?

When she becomes quiet I return to my paradise. My new friends are laughing and waving me over to join them. I inhale the most lovely fragrance as a melodic voice tells me, "In your new world, you have energy. You are safe from all harm, surrounded by peace and joy. Be free, you are strong. Have fun. Dance without legs, sing the notes of love."

I can only step so far and then I feel a tug at my back. I am not allowed to get any closer. I am in between worlds now. This one is of pain and sorrow where my body is locked, frozen in time. My mind is filled with frustration because I cannot make her stop crying. If I could speak, I would tell her I'm going to be okay. She must let go so that I can too.

The lab coat confirms that there will be no improvement. There is talk of removing life support. The whirring of machines is slowing. The up-and-down beep fades to a long, single tone and then stops altogether. This seems a somber time to those in the room, but for me it is a joyful release. I am finally able to move away from the bed, going higher. I am a bird that has been released from my cage. The ice has melted. I walk behind her. With both hands on her shoulders, I place a gentle kiss on the back of her neck. "Thank you," I say, not sure if she can hear me. As she presses both hands over her heart, I know that she has.

Again my misty friend speaks to me, "You speak without words. You feel total and unconditional love. Peace surrounds you as all other beings are there to support each other. You create with your thoughts. The wind is gentle and surrounds you like a blanket. Your eyes see beyond the walls." And at that point, I know I have returned home.

BABY TALK

"What kind of parent names their baby Brutus?" asked Ophelia.

"Someone with a strong connection to a past life in Rome apparently. But that's not the point," answered Ogden, her twin brother. "Watch him closely and you will see that he is new to the earth life."

Ogden and Ophelia had been at Kindertime Daycare for several weeks now and they were both beginning to feel pretty comfortable among their six-to-twelve-month-old peers. Ogden did not like this part of the re-entry to earth process because he was extremely experienced and found this floor crawling, mouth drooling, and total dependence on others to be a big waste of time. If he had his way, he would have entered the physical as a forty-year-old professor. He could start sharing his extensive knowledge right away and not spend his time like some helpless lump of chubby flesh. But this assignment was a little different. He came in with a twin sister this time. Ophelia had been here before, but struggled every time so the Master Guides thought it would be a good idea to send her in with a mentor.

Ophelia was both comforted and intimidated by her brother's experience. She knew she needed help in understanding the physical life that she had entered, but the pressure to succeed was overwhelming. This might be her last chance at incarnation and she didn't want to fail. The thought of spending eternity as a customer service representative at the Life Review

Center was enough to make her try even harder. The number of complaints that she received as the souls took a look at what they had accomplished (or in many more instances failed to achieve) was quite a bit more than one would imagine. She knew she was capable of contributing so much more.

"All I see is him eating his boogers," said Ophelia. "What am I supposed to learn from that?"

"Brutus is completely fixated on physical comfort. That's how you can tell he's never been here before," explained Ogden. "Now watch as he continues to drink from that bottle even when he is bursting."

"Okay, he's still eating. So what?"

"Wait for it . . ." He paused. "Wait for it . . . and there you have it," said Ogden as Brutus began to spit up the sour-smelling overflow all down the front of his onesie.

"Eww," said Ophelia as she wrinkled her nose and eyes.

"Eww, indeed," repeated Ogden. "He ate until he was full and then ate some more. Gluttony is not an attractive quality even in an eight-month-old."

Ophelia had much to learn. She reflected on the day they were first brought here. Ogden had told her it was important that she observe the behavior displayed in this temporary society of newly-arrived souls. It might help her to understand her role in their future life together.

————

"They are absolutely adorable!" squealed the Kindertime director. "I am so glad you chose our daycare for your precious babies. We'll take such good care of them, I promise." Leslie Fortner had been director for just over two years and was happy to see more babies arrive.

Jim and Joan Garner reluctantly handed over one baby each to the caregivers who stood with open arms.

"I'll take Ogden," said Jesse.

"And I'll hold Ophelia," said Louisa

Ogden Mark Garner and Ophelia May Garner were six months old and this was the first time they had been in someone else's care. They were a little skeptical, but Ogden had always stressed to Ophelia that she should embrace all learning experiences, wherever and whenever they took place. The two siblings had been communicating with each other for some time. Conveniently, no one else was aware of it.

"Speaking of names, how did we get such unusual names? I think it might be a little awkward as we get older," said Ophelia.

"Well, you may not remember, but when Dad found out he and Mom were about to be parents of twins, he said '*Oh my God! Oh my God!*' And so they thought it would be cute to give us those initials," said Ogden. "You know, OMG? I, for one, do not see the humor in it. It will be up to you how this impacts your future years, but trust me there will be more difficult things to have to work through."

"Like what?" she asked.

"Well, for starters you'll have to learn the nuances of their language. Then there's the unfortunate experience of teeth—perhaps the most maddening phase of our development. No matter how many chewy items they give you, it still hurts. There will be stumbling around like a drunken monkey, and don't get me started on how many dogs will lick the excess food from your face. Bedtimes are dictated whether you are tired or not, although I do appreciate a good naptime, and they will force you to expel your waste into a very large, water-filled bowl. They call it 'potty training.' Fair warning: they will applaud when you do it right," said Ogden with an air of revulsion.

"I think I remember some of that from last time. I'll adapt. With so much to cope with early on, why did we pick parents who would provide such a challenge for us right from the start?" asked Ophelia.

"I do have some ideas about that. For you, the answer will reveal itself over time. Focus now, we are moving on to our next example. See that one over there by the stuffed bear?" Ogden tried to point, once again frustrated at his inability to command his body parts.

"Sure, I see her. They call her Roxie. What can I learn from her?"

Louisa was holding some toys for Roxie to grab onto. The assistant was helping her to develop her motor skills. Every few minutes, though, she would wiggle her fingers over Roxie's tummy just to hear her giggle.

"Observe her obsession with tickling. She can't get enough of it," he said.

"Yes, Ogden, I hear her laughing all the time. I think that means she's happy, right? That's a good thing."

"I don't judge, I observe and report. She can reach her toes and when she does, she rolls over on her side. See. There she goes giggling again. Yesterday she told me how happy she was to be here."

"Isn't everyone?" asked Ophelia

"No, not everyone. But let's focus on Roxie for a moment, shall we? Her biggest asset as she develops into an adult human is her attitude. Notice the smile that seems to be so natural on her face. This will serve her well as she attempts to build on her physical experience. Not too many of the older ones maintain this feeling of joy throughout their lives. I have a good feeling about her, though."

"So you said that not everyone is happy to be here. Teach me about that," said Ophelia.

"We will continue tomorrow. It is naptime and I'm ready for my blanket," said Ogden as he rolled over and began to suck his thumb quietly.

"Aww, wisn't he a cutie wid his lidd'le blanky," said Jesse as she adjusted him in his little baby-cushion nest on the floor.

"My word woman, please don't talk to me like that. I'm not a baby!" Ogden thought to himself as he fell into a deep and dreamy sleep.

"Good morning all my precious children," said Leslie the next day. "Today we are going to have music in the day room." She and her assistants gathered their young charges and sat them in a semicircle facing a small piano.

"Oh no, I hate this activity. It is so boring," complained Ophelia.

"I actually appreciate this part of the day," said Ogden.

"Why? We can't do anything but sit here," said Ophelia.

"Exactly." But to his dismay, Ogden rolled over and could not right himself. Jesse saw him and placed some pillows on either side so he could stay sitting up. "Thank you," said Ogden, although it came out as "yan hoo" along with a little spit dripping off of his lower lip.

The director began pressing the keys and a lively melody came out. Jesse and Louisa added comical lyrics. Trying to be a good sport, Ophelia sat quietly as though she was paying attention. Roxie was clapping her hands against her thighs, laughing and rocking back and forth to the melody. Ophelia thought to herself, "What a show-off."

"So do you know why we sit and appreciate the music, Ophelia?" asked Ogden.

"Uh, no."

"Because we are honoring the creativity that music requires. It is important to validate the effort that was put into it."

"But it isn't that good. She's missing some notes and the singing is like an owl screeching in the night."

"That is exactly my point, Ophelia. It is not for us to determine whether an inspired activity is good or bad. It is, however, incumbent upon us to respect the attempt to create. You will need to cultivate your own form of creativity at some point as you progress. Remember this day as you begin to present your handiwork to the public," said Ogden, trying to impress upon his sister the importance of the artistic process.

"That's it? So, I've been finger-painting. Does that count?"

"It's a start," he responded. "There are a number of ways that will help you to build a practice of creating your own reality. By trying different methods, you will find what works best for you."

"Look—the twins are talking to each other again," said Louisa as she finished her song. "That is so sweet!"

"I'm trying to work here. Can we have a moment without one of you two trying to interrupt?" Ogden said in his own language. It was difficult enough going through this whole infantile process without having to train a lesser soul in the middle of a boo-boo party.

"Naptime, babies!"

"Well, there's a positive," thought Ogden.

———

"I just can't get used to that smell," complained Ophelia as Louisa sat her down in the reading circle.

"We are in agreement on that. I wish Brutus would make his doodoo before he left home in the morning," said Ogden. "Give us all a break."

"Did you make a poopy?" asked Jesse. "Let's take a look."

"No, he planted a rose garden in his diaper," growled Ogden. "When can we start properly describing what is happening here? Brutus loves the feel of it. Look at him. Like I said, he's new and can't get enough of these physical sensations. That baby has no dignity."

It was just after morning snack when Ogden felt some pressure in his tummy. He knew what he needed to do. As much as he hated being thrown over her shoulder like a sack of potatoes, he reached up to Louisa and whimpered. She bent over and picked him up, gently put him on her shoulder, and rubbed his back. He let out a nice burp and immediately felt better. He wanted to thank her, but after all, she was just doing her job. When he returned to his play space, Ophelia was waiting for him.

"I'm ready for another lesson," said Ophelia.

"Are you?" asked her brother as he picked at a plastic ball and unsuccessfully tried to throw it. The red sphere just fell from his fat fingers and barely made it to the end of his useless legs.

"A few days ago, you told me that some souls are not happy to be here."

"Yes, right," he said and then tried to kick the ball with a spastic foot. "Look at Timmy. He's staring at me, no expression—just staring."

"I don't see a problem there. He just looks bored," Ophelia said as she ran her hands down her dress. She liked the feeling of the ruffles.

"He is bored. And do you know why? Don't answer, I'll tell you why. Because he has no goals, no ambition, no purpose in his life." Ogden was annoyed with his inability to move the ball beyond his own toes.

"But he's just a baby," Ophelia protested. She caught her fingernail on a piece of trim on her dress and began to cry.

"Ophelia, what's the matter? Do you have an ouchie?" And with that, Louisa saw the finger snagged in the threads. She reached down and—with her mouth—bit the little offending nail. "That's better," she said as Ophelia stopped her little sobs.

"Oh, for astral sake. What passes for medical assistance around here is abhorrent."

"Tell me more about Timmy," said Ophelia after she recovered from her tiny injury. "Maybe we can help him."

"Oh, child, if it were only that easy. He must find his own way, but honestly he's not off to such a great start." Ogden was drained by this constant teaching of such an inexperienced soul. Why they picked him to escort her through this process was beyond him. She seemed like a nice person, but even with his superior guidance, it was doubtful that she would make it.

"Time for a movie, little ones!" said Jesse cheerfully. "Today we're going to watch . . ."

"Doesn't matter. Spoiler alert: Red's grandmother is really a bad wolf, Cinderella marries the prince, Bambi's mother dies—should I go on? I'd really like to see something a little more meaningful than these tired and depressing children's stories," Ogden snorted.

"So what would you suggest?" asked Ophelia.

"Well, *The Matrix* was always one of my favorites. Or how about *Inception*? These are movies that make you think, not make you cry."

"I'm going over to talk with Timmy. He looks like he needs a friend." Ophelia struggled to crawl toward him, so Louisa lifted her up and put her next to him.

"Hi there, Timmy. Why so quiet?"

"Crowds overwhelm me," he admitted.

"I get that," said Ophelia. "It's okay to want to have space. There is a lot going on here. Any thoughts about your future?" She wanted to prove that Ogden had been wrong about him.

"I'm going to be an explorer," said Timmy, happy to communicate with someone who was not trying to pressure him. "I plan to travel everywhere, see everything."

"Really? That sounds amazing. Tell me more about it," said Ophelia. She looked over toward Ogden to gauge his reaction, but a few moments earlier he had leaned against a big floor pillow and was snoring quietly. He was such a paradoxical little man.

The twins had been at Kindertime now for more than six months. Ophelia felt like her lessons were coming along fairly well. With Ogden's guidance she was much more confident about her ability to have a successful growth experience. She understood why Langley cried all the time—he had to leave his soul mate behind on the astral as part of their agreement. It would take him some time to forget and dive in to his new life.

Ogden explained that Carlotta's curiosity was part of her desire to make an important discovery; she was practicing for her future self. And knowing that the director, Leslie, could not have children of her own explained why her job of caring for children was so important to her.

There was just one thing that was nagging at her. She felt like there was something that she needed to accomplish but couldn't quite put her fat little finger on it.

"Ogden?"

"Yes, Ophelia?" Ogden responded as he was practicing his stance. His legs were finally gaining some strength and he knew a few steps forward might be just days away. He held onto the toy box next to him and lifted his right foot up, steady, steady and down. Ogden fell right on his well-padded bottom. "I shall try again tomorrow," he thought to himself, trying to move past the embarrassment of the whole situation.

"I think I'm starting to forget where I came from. It scares me," Ophelia said in her softest voice.

"I understand. One thing you need to know is that as we begin to learn their language and start thinking in their words, our origin memory begins to fade." He sat with his hands on his knees as though his fall had been intentional.

"Is there anything we can do to stop it?"

"Some have tried, but it is important to begin your assimilation. There will be sacrifices, but that's how we learn."

"Do you have any advice for me before I lose my thoughts of home?"

"Well, yes. This is generally reserved for those who have been here for more linear time, but maybe if you meditated on it, you could retrieve the important parts," said Ogden. "During our next nap time, you could focus all of your energy on identifying the mission of your journey here."

"Really? I can do that?"

"I suspect you can based on what I've taught you," Ogden said as he noticed a stream of stickiness coming from his nose. "Angels have mercy, can I get a tissue?" Looking around for help, he was even more motivated now to walk on his own.

After lunch, Louisa and Jesse set up all the little baby nap cushions around the room, dimmed the lights and played some lullaby music. Timmy was quiet, already dreaming about his next expedition. Roxie was smiling in her sleep with visions of balloons, ice cream, and ponies. Ophelia glanced at Ogden to make sure he was sleeping and saw his arms and legs spread across the pillows. She could see that he would soon need something bigger to sleep in. The timing was perfect to attempt meditation. She was determined to get a message from her source.

"Ppphhhiitttt." Brutus was making noises from his butt again, but soon settled down to wherever his dreams were taking him.

"I am aware," she repeated in her head. With Ogden's instructions in mind, she continued. "My mission is clear. I will remember my purpose for this incarnation." Her brown curls began to bounce as her head nodded forward.

When an hour had passed, Jesse used the dimmer switch to adjust the lights and the room gradually became brighter. Louisa gave each child a gentle nudge. "Wake up, you little sleepy heads. Time for a walk."

Ogden thought it a cruel promise as he knew their idea of a walk was sitting in a stroller and riding up and down the front sidewalk. He was not impressed, but at least it was fresh air. They loaded Timmy next to Roxie,

Ogden next to Ophelia, and Brutus had a row to himself in the six-seat stroller. Even without proper language, Jesse instinctively knew that no one wanted to sit with gassy Brutus.

Ophelia looked over to her brother and smiled, remembering the message she received during her meditation.

"You have been placed with Ogden to show him tolerance, patience, and humility. You will do this for a lifetime as his student, sister, and confidante. Use your thoughts, words, and deeds. You may forget some of the details, but you will always remember your mission."

This was a purpose that she looked forward to achieving because in just about a year she had learned to love him and vowed to look after him for the rest of her life.

THE BEAUTIFUL SCAR

Her son lived only in her heart now, steeped in memories, shrouding her in the worst grief imaginable. She was consumed by the knowledge that she would never see him again, never cook his favorite meals, or watch *Game of Thrones* together. She would never see him walk across the stage accepting a diploma, never be the proud mother of the groom, and never have the chance to be a doting grandmother to his children. Every life event that they would miss spending together brought her grief to the surface with a gut punch.

She faked her way through each day, telling people she was fine and yes, time did heal all wounds. But inside she was filled with unrelenting sorrow—sometimes she wondered how she would even get through the day without totally falling apart. She had become quite clever at hiding her pain, as she knew that her friends and even family had tired of hearing her melancholy tone. Invitations to events became fewer and fewer as no one seemed to want to be around her non-stop sadness. And that was a welcome change, as she had grown weary of the insensitive comments. "He's in a better place." "Heaven needed another angel." And worst of all, "You are young, you can have another child."

Shortly after the death of her son, Sheila joined a grief-support group. In the beginning, she just liked being around people where she could be herself. No pretense of strength, they were all hurting. Tears were not only shared freely but expected. They talked through all the stages of grief and how long before each of the participants would "get over it" and "move on with their lives." When you lose a child these were unlikely scenarios. Their facilitator talked about exercise and journaling, making memorials, and learning new hobbies.

It quickly became an irrelevant exercise as one would ask the group, "How long should I wait before dating again?" Others were concerned about disposing of their parent's belongings. No one, it seemed, could relate to the crushing grief of losing a child and frankly she was in no position to support anyone else in the circle. It was time to try something new.

With urging from a cousin she went to her pastor. Father Frank was kind and soft spoken. He quoted Isaiah 43:2, "God will carry you through the storm," and told her to have faith. They sat together and prayed. There was some comfort in believing that her beautiful son was in heaven, but it did not resolve the persistent ache associated with his short life and violent death. After several visits from the church ladies auxiliary, she told him she was fine and no longer required the counsel. Thank you so much, I feel better now. Not.

Sheila continued to seek out some real support. There must be someone who would understand, someone she could talk to who would help her to see the purpose in all of this pain.

––––––––

"Tell me about Kevin," he said. This new counselor was different. He asked questions rather than tell her how she should feel. She met with him in the evening, in her home. Sheila was not sure how these sessions began, but she was comfortable with him, feeling like maybe he was someone who could really help her. This was a spiritual man. She could feel it deep in her soul. When asked, he had said, "Just call me Stanley." She thought her son would have approved of this new approach.

"He was kind, always asking our elderly neighbors if they needed anything. He liked to visit and listen to their stories about growing up in the 30s and 40s. Sometimes he would go to the market with them just to reach for the items on a higher shelf or to help carry their groceries from the car into the house."

"Sounds like a thoughtful young man. He seems to have been a very supportive person, helping others without thought of repayment. That speaks well of his character. Did he have any hobbies?"

"Kevin was quiet, but creative. He played the guitar. Self-taught," she beamed with pride. "He drew with colored pencils—mostly cartoon characters, but I knew he was destined to take his art to the next level." Her eyes became teary again thinking of the lost opportunity to watch him grow into his talent.

"I think about him every day. In my mind's eye, I am picturing him at home with us. I still ask him out loud what he would like me to fix for his school lunch. I tell him about the neighbors, and ask if he has finished his homework."

"Do you think that you may be subtly encouraging him to live in his past? You could be affecting his future by trying to keep his consciousness here in the physical." It was a direct and potentially painful comment, but it needed to be said.

"His future? The animal that shot him on the street just to get his cell phone eliminated any future for him." She was getting angry now at this man who had clearly never experienced a loss of this magnitude. But he continued in spite of her frustration.

"Just because he is not in the physical doesn't mean he has lost the ability to grow. He still has much to learn and he can only do that by balancing his energy between the earthly world that he shared with you and the nonphysical life that he now leads."

"Are you saying that I am interfering with the growth of my son?"

"You are both in a development phase, a time when change has come and a different approach may be considered. Rather than continue to grieve the loss of his physical being, consider how to embrace a new kind of relationship," said Stanley.

"But I loved him so much. It's not so easy just to let him go." She was once again angry that someone who had never felt this pain dared to give her advice.

"You don't have to let go of the love you shared."

"Why does this love have to hurt so badly?" she asked him as she grabbed a pillow and squeezed it hard.

"That is the perplexing orbit of emotion. Your grief is intense because your love was intense. Would you choose to give up one so you would not feel the other?" He challenged her with this line of thought.

Maybe this therapist was no better than the others. Was he saying that she should abandon her son and just move on? Perhaps she would never find the peace that she needed so badly, but she had to keep trying. Shelia closed her eyes and leaned back into the softness of her couch. She was exhausted.

During their next session Stanley decided to use a different tactic. "Where do you think he is now? In your mind what is he doing?" He sat forward to bring focus to his question.

"I don't know. I call to him. Every day I ask him to contact me, to send me a sign to let me know he is okay. Part of my anxiety is that I don't know where he is or what he is doing."

"Let me ask this another way. Rather than speculate, tell me what you think he would be doing if he had total freedom to pursue anything he wanted. Picture the things that Kevin would be enjoying as he expands his spiritual presence in the universe."

"I suppose that he would be creating more artwork, using the tools that can only be found outside of the physical. Maybe he would be learning to play more instruments . . ." Sheila spoke to him in a thoughtful way after she considered Kevin's future in these terms.

"You can say it. He has more creative prospects on the astral plane. He has no limits when given the opportunity to try anything."

"Yes, I suppose." She didn't sound totally convinced and frankly it was difficult to imagine that Kevin would no longer need her. Sheila did not want to talk anymore, so she ended her time with Stanley and fixed herself some tea.

———

"Well, what do you think? Is she getting any closer?" Kevin spoke to Stanley with the impatience of a teenager.

"She is beginning to think about it, but we still have a long way to go. I told you when I took this on that the most intense heartache is that of a parent who has lost a child," Stanley reminded him.

"I feel so bad for her. This is my fault. If I hadn't been out later than my curfew, it would never have happened and she wouldn't be in so much pain."

"Kevin, you must release that thought and the energy behind it. There is no blame to be assigned. If not this incident, it would have been something else that brought you home. Attachment to the past works as a restriction in both the physical and spiritual worlds. Your dependence on each other is keeping you both from evolving as spiritual beings."

"I'm not sure how I can just let go. This guilt keeps pulling me back to our physical house even though I know I must have more to accomplish here."

"Understand that the two of you were walking together for a period of linear time. Your physical death puts you both at a fork in the road. Now you each have the opportunity to follow a separate-but-parallel course for your next lessons. Focus on the present, on your current life prospects. I'm going to invite your mother to our group conference session. You should listen in on the discussion. I'm hoping that will work for both of you." With that promise, Stanley faded from Kevin's view.

"I cannot make you feel better. There is nothing I, or anyone else for that matter, can say that will take away your pain. Sheila, you are a spiritually advanced human or we would not be having this conversation. You know that we do not die, but continue on in other forms." He paused to let her absorb his latest comment. "I think you might benefit from a class that I am teaching tomorrow night. Do you think you can be there? There will be some others in the audience who have had similar experiences."

Shelia nodded that she would be interested and fully intended to be there. She fell asleep early. In her next conscious thought, Shelia found herself sitting in a mid-size hotel conference room. There were chairs lined up across the floor, all facing a small stage along one wall. She had a clear view of the speaker and in a few moments, she saw Stanley going through some sheets of paper on the podium. "I must be at the group meeting he talked about," she thought. It didn't surprise her that she didn't remember the drive. Most days were still foggy like that.

"I want to thank you all for coming here tonight. Some of what I say may be hard to hear. But you have chosen to take this next step and for that I commend you," Stanley addressed the room. Sheila felt the presence of others although it was hard to see any details. She decided to just focus on his words.

"Let me begin by asking you a question. How do you remember your loved one? Someone who left dirty dishes on the counter or snored in the movie theater? Perhaps they always forgot your birthday, or spent too much time online?" He paused for effect. "No? Of course not. We tend to think of the good times and special moments—family celebrations and personal achievements. In general, we do not want to remember our loved one in an unpleasant light." Some remarks rippled through the audience.

"So think about this. What if the same is true for them? As your loved one watches over you, they do not want to observe a sad, sick, inactive mother, but a vibrant presence appreciative of living. She would be joyful and energetic with a strong purpose in life."

It was a question that really hit home for her. Sheila thought, "Is he talking to me?"

"So how do we get there? After such tragedy, how can we return to the person they remember, that they loved, the person that they laughed with?" Stanley waited for a moment, turned over a page on the podium, and then returned his attention to the crowd.

"Grief changes us from the mother, husband, or child we once were. Often it is driven by the mystery surrounding death. They were here and now they are gone. What just happened? We sometimes have a tendency to be in control—to be caretakers—to comfort and protect those who have been placed in our charge. When they die, it is as if we have failed. Consider this: it may have been our assignment all along to be that protector for just a finite period of time. This is especially true as a parent."

Sheila knew he was speaking directly to her. She looked down at her hands and began to bite at a cuticle that was coming loose.

"Society tells us that it is our job to provide basic necessities for our children—food, shelter, love, education. As they get older we are mentoring them into adulthood so that they will be successful on their chosen path. If they do not stay in the physical timeline as we had planned, then somehow we believe that we have been unsuccessful as the custodian of their soul."

Sheila wiped a tear from her cheek, totally connecting to his observation. She did feel like she had failed Kevin, that she had not protected him from the dangers of the world.

"It is important to recognize that you have provided exactly what was needed. It is likely that the lesson during this incarnation was completed. Rather than feeling guilt, perhaps you should feel satisfaction that you have done your job—realized your mutual objective. Are you looking forward to their next opportunity for growth? Of course you are. But you must realize that in some cases, it may not happen physically with you."

"That sounds easier than it is. Losing a child is incomprehensively painful." This comment came from the back of the room from a faceless participant. "Why do we have to experience such torment?"

"We know that we are in the physical world to learn. The truth is that many lessons include angry situations, unfulfilled dreams, emotional pain, and the longing that comes when a loved one has moved on without us. This is the conflict that jolts you into a learning experience."

"How do we reconcile this conflict without abandoning our children?" added another voice from the room.

"And there is our challenge. There is a way to maintain communication without interrupting the progress of our spiritual evolution. I will cover that with each of you in your individual sessions."

Returning home, Sheila was struggling to retain what Stanley had talked about during the conference. Her higher self, her inner guidance, knew he was right. Everything was logical to her now, but still it hurt.

"Do you mean just get over it? Get on with our life as though it never happened?" Shelia thought to herself.

"This is not a call to get over anything," Stanley responded to her thoughts. "Our physical existence will never be the same; no one expects you to erase that part of your life. But the fact is that change has come. That is something we can accept—adapting in the best way we know how—or deny and stay miserable, locked in the past."

"So what can I do?" Sheila found herself pacing, crossing her arms over her chest as if protecting her broken heart from further damage.

"What is your favorite memory of Kevin?" Stanley knew that Kevin was watching, so he changed his slant.

"That's easy. It was his twelfth birthday party. When we were deciding on invitations, he wanted to include his entire class. He knew that there were kids in his school that never got invited to parties and he didn't want anyone to feel left out."

"Kevin is very special," said Stanley emphasizing the present tense.

"And he told everyone that instead of bringing gifts for him, he wanted to donate everything to the children's hospital program. He even went so far as to get a recommended gift list from the nurse's station. I have never been so proud." Shelia smiled for the first time in many days.

"Suppose I told you that because of that day, one bullied child who had considered ending his life became hopeful for his future. Another one—a little girl in the hospital—will grow up to discover a ground-breaking medical treatment for children's cancer because an unexpected gift gave her the motivation to help others. There was a dad who did not drink and drive after a baseball game that day because he had to take his son to the first birthday party he had ever been invited to."

"I had no idea."

"Most people don't."

"Mom, you inspired me to think beyond myself from when I was very young," Kevin whispered.

Sheila looked over Stanley's shoulder. "Kevin?"

"I'm here. I've been watching you and it makes me sad to see you in so much pain. This is totally my fault."

"No. Don't feel that way. I don't blame you for anything." Through her tears Sheila tried to reassure him, to help ease the pain he had carried since the incident. "But you're okay now?"

"I'm more than okay. I've been surrounded by love and grace, peace and kindness. There are endless creative possibilities here. But it is hard to participate in anything because I feel so bad for you. I wanted you to be happy again, so I sent Stanley. He's an astral counselor."

"So we can keep talking? You can give me updates on what you are doing? Maybe send me signs during the day so I'll know you are still doing well?"

"Yes, of course, but maybe in a more positive way. Stanley assures me that we can still have a relationship as long as we don't become more focused on each other than on our own paths of evolution. We need to develop a plan so that we can retain our independence as we stay connected on this deeper level." Stanley was quite impressed with Kevin's comment. He really did understand.

"When you died, my heart was torn open and exposed to the coldest air, the sharpest pain. I will never forget it, never forget you. I have a deep scar that will never heal." Kevin did not know how to respond in words, so he looked over at Stanley for help.

"You shouldn't forget and couldn't if you tried. Scars are the result of a wound. Wounds heal, but the scar remains. Scars are part of our story. They can be a reminder of what we have achieved, what we have overcome, what we have learned. And yours is beautiful," added Stanley in his ethereal voice.

"I feel your absence in the depth of my soul Kevin. I can't promise to be happy, but maybe I can be a little less sad now that I know you are safe," said Sheila. And then she turned her comment to Stanley. "You said we could maintain some kind of communication that will help us both." She waited for a response from their counselor.

"During an out-of-body experience, meditation or lucid dream, you need only to ask for Kevin's presence."

"I've asked for messages from a psychic, but I never know if it is truly real. Sometimes there are key words that make sense, phrases that give me some kind of confirmation; but I must admit that I would rather have a direct conversation."

"Psychics can provide a valuable service when giving comfort to someone who is grieving, but you are now ready to do this yourself. And just as important, so is Kevin. You both need to create boundaries and give each other space to grow into your next phases of life," added Stanley.

"Mom, I'll always love you. We will see each other again when it is right for us both, but you should know that I have more work to do here. Remember, I am at my best when you are living your brightest life, one that has meaning and purpose."

"I get it. It is time for me to embrace this next part of my life and to meet the challenges for my own growth. But can you at least give me a sign now and then that you are doing well? Can you show me that you are sometimes thinking of me?" Sheila arranged with her son to keep some kind of connection.

"Every time you hear someone strumming a guitar, sense that I am with you, sending love to you," Kevin said to his mother. "And when you need to talk to me, I promise to listen."

"I think I can do that. There aren't too many places around here where people play guitars, but I can see that as a sign from you when I do hear them. And if you see me looking through your art projects, will you think of me as well?"

"You know I will."

"Now that you have established your connection plan, I will leave you both to your next steps." Stanley's sessions were over, so he left them to the work that would follow.

"Thank you Stanley," said Shelia. "Now I know Kevin is well and I can remain in his life; I just need to take a step back and allow him to follow his path."

"Thank you, Mom, for everything. I'll talk to you soon," added Kevin.

Sheila felt her breath catch in her throat as she emitted a short gasp. She rose from her bed when the sensation in her arms and legs returned and noticed that she was feeling just a little better. Once dressed, she ran her fingers through her hair and grabbed the car keys for an important errand. The sign that said *Administrative Office of Green County Community College* included an arrow that directed her to the next parking lot. The walk to the office was refreshing and it felt good to stretch her legs; it was as if she was on a mission.

"Do you have any music students who need a scholarship to continue their education?" she asked the young man behind the counter.

"Why yes, we do. The string section students could use some assistance. Actually, there is a fund-raising concert this weekend," he responded.

"I would love to attend the concert. And where do I sign up to make a contribution to the scholarship fund?" Sheila pulled her checkbook out as she thought about her beautiful son and how he continued to do good things for people even after he was gone from this world.

That night, as she said her evening gratitude affirmations, she added a comment to her son about the weekend concert. She heard his response very quietly: "I'll be there, too.

WEEKEND AT THE AKASHIC

"Welcome to the Akashic Inn!"

The door was thrown open upon my approach and I was greeted by an old man who bared some missing teeth in his one-sided grin. While one hand stroked the long white beard, his other reached out to grab mine. He revealed surprising strength as he pulled me into the foyer. I later learned that this was an assessment area where the guardians of The Akashic made a determination about the length of your stay. His silky white robes swirled around his legs just enough so I could see his blue-satin embroidered slippers.

"Well, well. You want to see about your past lives, eh?" He looked me over head to toe and then slowly spun me around to see me in a three-hundred-sixty-degree view. I was beginning to wonder if I had made a mistake coming here. "Why?" he asked me with his head at a slight tilt.

"Why? Because I'm curious."

"Not good enough," he said. "Try again."

"I want to know who I was, what kind of person I was in the past, before my current physical life."

"Why?"

"Because it seems that my romantic relationships don't end well. Commitment issues, I've been told. There. I said it. Someone suggested that it might be a past-life thing, so here I am." This guy was not the welcoming guide that I had expected.

"That's better," he said. "We get too many tourists here, just looking around trying to see what's what, and they never intend to use the information to make changes."

"Well then, can I ask you a question?" I couldn't let his gruff attitude sway me from learning as much as I could.

"I'm sure there will be more than one, but yes, go ahead."

"Why do you look like a wizard? It's so cliché!"

"That's what you expect to see, so that's what you see. Actually, it's our most popular look. Everybody thinks their guide is a wise old man with a long white beard, wearing white silky robes. But, if you'd rather that I be a troll or an alien, or what do you young folks like? Zombies? Yes, I can do that too. Maybe you want to see angel wings?" And with that, two plumes sprung out from his back.

"No. I'm okay with the whole wizard thing. Let's stick with that."

"Okay, then," he said as he swiftly recreated his original form. "Take your bags, go through the main hall down the aisle on your right, and then go up two flights of stairs. When you get to the top make a left, walk past six doors, and you'll see a piece of art with some stars on it. It will be crooked. Straighten it and then stomp your foot three times. The door that opens is where your path will begin."

"Is all that really necessary?"

"Like I said before, too many tourists. We have to know that you are willing to put in the work."

"Got it," and I started to make my way through the main hall. I regretted bringing two suitcases, but I didn't know what to expect. I was trying to prepare for whatever came up by bringing my stuff, but what I failed to see was that I didn't need any of it.

Up the stairs, past the six doors, I straightened the painting and obediently stomped my feet. Suddenly before me was an opening that led me to an outside garden. A distant bell rang and I felt very sleepy. I could smell freshly baked bread. Drawn to a staircase by a nearby stone wall, I decided that some important part of my story was about to appear.

I begin to hear other voices. I have become a stocky man with hair sparsely scattered in a ring from ear to ear around the back of my head. I wear wool robes in shades of brown and tan. At first, I believe myself to be a monk, but then I realize that I have flour sprinkled generously on an apron that covers my cloak from the waist down. At the bottom of the stairs is a short walkway. I follow that to an open door where I can hear the buzz of group activity. I enter and hear my name. "Barr, you're back. We don't have much time before dinner. Do you have the biscuits ready?" I become this man who is being called to the kitchen and know that my name is Bartholomew, but everyone who knows me calls me Barr—Barr the Baker.

"Yes, everything will be on the tray when you need it," I answer cheerfully. I love my job baking for the royal court. We are in the late Middle Ages. The queen enjoys my cookies, cakes, and breads and it such an honor to be working in her service. She is kind and loved by all for her generous nature and impartial way of handling disagreements in the village.

"Evalyn," I plate up the baked goods and pass it to my daughter who has just turned fifteen. She is not yet a woman but grown enough to join us in serving the royal family. She has been given the assignment of bringing food to the lesser tables in the main dining room. I want to make sure she looks the part and is not late with any of the trays. There was room

for advancement and I wanted to make sure she did well in her training.

"Yes, father. I'm on my way."

It has been a struggle since her mother died. Claudia was my beloved wife. We worked together here in the castle, she with the seamstress and I in the kitchen. She died when Evalyn was very young. After she was gone, I gave up my apartment to live in a sparse room off of the kitchen hallway. I have a stone bed, softened by old blankets that are no longer used in the upper chambers. A small desk and chair in the corner double as a dining table for one. As a senior member of the staff, I have a 2 x 4 window in my room, just big enough let in some fresh air and sunlight.

Thankfully, the kind ladies in the kitchen have helped to raise my precious Evalyn. When she was little, she was often spotted running around the kitchen and nabbing the broken pieces of cakes and cookies. As she got older, the kitchen women tried to train her in the ways of the castle and I taught her to cook. She generally stayed with them and we all worked together as they formed a surrogate family for my energetic little girl. Romantically, there was never another woman for me after Claudia. I focused all my attention on serving my queen and raising my daughter.

I am rolling out some cookies with a block rolling pin. On each side, the royal seal is carved into squares. As I press this into the dough, the seal impression is made. I cut the squares and place them on a baking sheet. This is a new item and I am hoping the queen likes my effort.

As usual Evalyn returns from her serving duty and brings a plate of leftovers to me. She is concerned that I am not eating well and wants to make sure I keep up my strength. The gout has begun to take its toll on me. Some days it is very difficult to walk, so it was a good plan to teach my daughter to bake.

One night right before the evening meal, a messenger is sent to the pantry informing everyone that the queen wishes to see me. I am not sure why this request has been made, but I know I must hurry. I wash my hands and try to cool down my face, which has been turning red from all the years spent in the heat of the kitchen.

"Your majesty." I try to bow, but my knees are swollen and I am a round fellow from trying out my new cake recipes. She doesn't seem to mind.

"Bartholomew of the . . ." The queen leans in to her advisor and nods. She sits forward again and faces me.

"Bartholomew of the countryside, I present to you this ribbon of service as a token of honor and loyalty. For twenty-five years you have been a faithful servant and gifted baker. For this the court is pleased."

"Thank you, my queen." My second attempt at bowing is not much more successful than the first. There is some scattered applause in the hall and I am ushered out and back to the kitchen. The kitchen ladies are excited to hear every detail, but the only thing that matters to me is that Evalyn is proud of her father.

More time passes and Evalyn is now a lovely 17-year-old woman. I know that it is time for her to be with a husband and I am pleased that she has developed feelings for one of the queen's guard. His name is Dinar and with my blessing, they marry in the side yard by a beautiful spring growth of pink rose bushes. Evalyn has rolled up my ribbon of honor and loyalty, putting it in her pocket for good luck.

Because they are both employed by the queen, they are given a small apartment in the castle. I miss her running around my dough tables. The kitchen is a little quieter without her. I lost my wife at a young age and now my daughter is moving away from the life I made for her. I know she will be safe and no longer needs me, so I will leave this life as I have no more obligation to it. Several weeks after the wedding, I die in my sleep. My heart just stopped beating. I am met by Claudia.

"Do you have any regrets from this life?" I can hear someone asking me in a distant voice.

"Just that I did not leave a better life for my daughter," I answered with a lump forming in my throat.

"Evalyn will be happy and safe. We could not ask for a better life than that," my wife responded to my thoughts.

"What would you recognize as your accomplishments in this life?"

"That I raised my daughter with love and served my queen well." I answered the voice in my head.

"Have you forgotten about the ribbon?"

"Honor and Loyalty." Then I held my wife close to me and faded away.

I began to drowsily return to the present day and saw that the wizard was seated in the garden. He drank from a glass of what appeared to be lemonade, while a second glass waited for me across the table. He motioned for me to join him and offered me a notebook. I quickly took notes so that I wouldn't forget anything, even drawing pictures of the hedges and gate marking the boundary of the castle grounds.

"So now that you have been given the details of a past life, it might be helpful to look at it in terms of your current life." He encouraged me to take some time and see if there were any parallels that I could draw. "These comparisons are neither good nor bad, they just are."

"I did a good job taking care of others, even got a ribbon for loyalty. Perhaps I should have looked more into my own needs."

"Only you know that for sure."

"I remember that the two most important people in my life left me. Maybe that's why I have a hard time with commitment."

"You've had many lives. Often, there is more going on in your consciousness than what you can see in your physical world. But now it's time for you to take a well-deserved break. I've arranged for you to have a massage with one of our premier therapists. She'll meet you in the main hall. Enjoy!" And he raised his glass in a toast.

I gathered my notebook and said goodbye. I was quite impressed with his newly displayed generosity. A carved sign that read "Soul Spa" appeared as the garden seemed to fade away. The glass-paneled door easily swung open for me.

As I am following the soft music and the skilled hands of the therapist, I become totally relaxed. About halfway through the session, I feel like we had been joined by a nonphysical presence. She is a woman in her mid-thirties with a pale but flawless complexion. In contrast, her eyes are heavily shadowed and thick with black mascara. Red lips form a circle around an ivory cigarette holder. She tilts her head slightly backward to expel smoke up toward the ceiling. Sitting on the arm of a chair upholstered in faded cabbage rose with her legs crossed, she is gently twirling her right foot to the tune of the music. Her thick blond hair is lifted high up on the center of her head with the sides falling straight down just brushing

the top of her broad-shouldered suit jacket. It is made in soft-
pink wool and matches her knee-length skirt, reminding me of
how a woman would dress in the 1940s.

I felt like we had been visited by a soul from a previous existence but I was certain that it was not me. Maybe it was the past life of Amalie, my massage therapist. As soon as that thought came into my mind, I felt sharp pains in my stomach area. The session ended a few minutes later. As she was gathering towels and other equipment, she casually asked me how it felt and when I relayed my vision, she stopped and turned to me. "You just described my persona in a past life. The pain you had? Well, in that life I had died during childbirth." As her words were spoken a movie played against the white wall. I began watching. It was of me and my first hours of life. As I was born, my mother died.

It was then I realized Amalie was also a guest at the inn. It was clear that I needed to feel her pain and that she had to have some acknowledgement that her experience had been real. The guardians had engaged us in a situation to facilitate the growth and knowledge of each other. There was a connection now between the two of us. It seemed like I should feel some regret, some guilt about what had happened to her, but I didn't. Instead, I felt that I had healed an old wound. I hoped I would see her again while I was here.

"What was that about?" I asked the wizard when we met again around the fireplace.

"Your experience is based on your personal quest. I don't have control in that regard, only you can direct your journey while you are here. Remember this is a place of collective memories, the history of all things."

"Why do people reincarnate?" I asked the wizard. "It seems like once you know how difficult life can be, well, you would just stay on the astral and enjoy your freedom to create."

"There is no straightforward explanation to your inquiry," he responded as he brought his prayer hands to his lips. "There are many reasons for reincarnation: lessons to be learned, experiences to be lived, challenges to be met, karmic scales to be balanced, rationalization for current life behaviors, regrets, and even something as simple as boredom. You may take a rest now and we will continue again later."

I had become quite thirsty, so I went to the kitchen seeking a beverage. "I wonder if I can get a cold beer in this place," I thought.

My name now is Marta and I am in a tavern with three mugs of beer in each hand, making my way through a dozen long wooden tables. My full hips are magnified by a red ankle-length skirt, the front half of which is covered with an earth-toned apron pulled tightly around the gathered waist. The corseted vest that squeezes my waist and keeps my white peasant blouse in place has embroidered ribbons around the sides and bottom. With each step, my skirts brush against either the customers or the tables. As many as eight men at every table are equally laughing, pounding the table with the bottom of a closed fist, and slapping their tablemates on the back.

I find my destination and put all six mugs down on the table. 'Here's another round gentlemen. This should keep you quenched for a few minutes, anyway.' There is more laughter and murmurs of appreciation as I weave myself through the crowd back to the bar to pick up another order.

I own this tavern with Helmut, my husband of nine years. He looks over at me and smiles as he services the customers at the bar. I remember that we were happy with our choice to take over this place when his uncle died. We even kept the same name, 'Kutcher's Wirthaus.' The small apartment over the tavern was all we needed as we had remained childless. But it was alright because were always busy and spent our days pleasing others and serving the community where we lived. We hired local townspeople during the busiest season and always had a hot meal for those who were unable to pay.

One night while I am cleaning up behind the bar, a man comes in through the closed doors. Why hadn't Helmut locked up as he swept the floor earlier this evening? I look into his shiny black eyes and notice that he doesn't look like our typical customer. His facial hair is neatly trimmed, his shirt looks clean. Looking down, I see that his pants are pressed and his boots are polished. Something makes me uncomfortable, but we have a rule to never turn anyone away that needs to eat—even if they aren't obviously poor. You could never tell about someone's current circumstance. 'We're closed for the evening, but I can get you some cold meat if you're hungry.' He walks slowly toward me and I wish that Helmut was still here. He had insisted on taking tonight's leftover stew to the Friedrich family down the street.

'Money,' is all he says as he stabs me. My last thoughts are of regret that Helmut would find me here like this and that his life would never be the same.

"Now look deeper. Remember why you are here. You had questions about your current ability to make a relationship work." The wizard was standing by my side as I began to regain a sense of my physical being. "This is another previous life where I see that you left your partner at a relatively young age."

I was beginning to see a pattern where my relationships ended abruptly due to circumstances that I could not control. I went outside and began to follow a walking path to another building.

I am about five years old, hiding behind a porch column in front of a one-room shack of a house. Built with mud and straw like the dozens of others that lined the dirt road, it is home to a poor family. My dress is ragged and dirty, made from old burlap sacks, and my hair has not been combed in days. I can feel the grime between the toes of my bare feet. Many of the villagers are outside in anticipation of a parade of some kind down the main street of town.

In minutes, I see who is coming—soldiers wearing the same uniforms as those who had killed my mother. They are wearing tall hats, pretty red jackets with shiny brass buttons, and tight white pants tucked into knee-high black boots. Some march in rows. I see a group approaching my house. They accompany a cannon rolling on wheels so high, they are taller than me. When I see my chance, I reach under my torn skirts, grab a knife, and run into the street. I stab the nearest soldier in the back of his leg as many as three or four times before he turns and slams my head into the wooden wheel of the cannon wagon.

I fall limp onto the street. I am dead.

"Whoa. That was intense," I thought as my legs still felt weak from reliving the experience.

"Life does not have to be long in order to have a meaningful impact. Are you beginning to see any answers to the questions you had upon your arrival?" asked the wizard.

"Yes. I see that I have a long history of relationships that are out of my control. They end abruptly and in many cases far too early."

"Linear time is irrelevant. It seems that you are allowing your expectations to overshadow the purpose of the experience."

"I don't understand," I said to him.

"When you enter a relationship you have preconceived ideas about what will make it successful." I hadn't seen her arrive, but Amalie was there providing support to me, almost advising me like a mother would to her son. "Those are not always met, so you think something has gone wrong. In fact, most involvement with others can provide a learning experience, even if those unions are not long in earth time." With Amalie's return, I was beginning to see how we are all interconnected.

"That is correct," said the wizard. "You may desire an outcome that does not support the lesson you are there to receive. For example, you wished for Claudia to live as your wife for many more years than she did. If not for her departure, you would not have had the same relationship with your daughter."

"The depth of your involvement is far more important than the length of time spent in it," added Amalie.

"As a child you lost your life at the hand of a soldier. What you did not see is that the action you took drew notice to the plight of your town. As a result, living conditions began to improve for everyone." The wizard brought this to my attention because I would never have seen it otherwise.

"Now I get it. I may think a relationship is short-lived, but it might be just the exact right amount of time. There may be other circumstances at play. It's a big-picture thing," I said and as the words came out of my mouth, my suitcases appeared. I got the hint. My weekend was over.

"At the Akashic Inn, you can find details on everything from a minor incident to a major event and everything else in between. You are welcome back anytime you need guidance, information, or insights about your spiritual evolution." The wizard rattled off the sales pitch that was on the brochure.

I picked up my luggage for my return trip and noticed that the bags were noticeably lighter. My consciousness moved from the Akashic Inn to my apartment in a flash of time. As soon as I returned to the physical, I knew I had a phone call to make.

"So, welcome back. How was your weekend?" she asked. Someone was glad to hear my voice.

"It was . . . enlightening," I said, answering with the only way I could describe it. "I'd like to see you tonight. There are some things I'd like to talk about."

My life had just become brighter and less complicated and I was more open to embrace whatever was to happen next.

LIFE BOAT

"All gassed up and ready to go." Doug closed the fuel cap on the
Mercury engine. He readied the Bimini top that provided the overhead
shade. It was a little overcast; the clouds were swirling briskly across the
sky. But he knew that when the spring sun did come out, having the canvas in place would provide some shelter from the glare that bounced off
the water.

"Hey, Mom, I've got the sunscreen and the bug spray," Sara added.

"I have drinks, apples, cookies and napkins," said Ella as she joined
her husband and children on their 24-foot pontoon boat.

"I'm not wearing that stupid life jacket!" Jack said as he stomped his
foot. The boy was five and eager to get the summer started, even though
they had just celebrated St. Patrick's Day the previous week. He always
resisted wearing his life vest until his nine-year-old sister convinced him
that pirates wore them. "How do you think they survived in the high seas?"
she asked him. Wise beyond her years, Sara often jumped in to mediate
family disputes.

Even though she had a nagging thought that being out on the water
today was a bad idea, Ella agreed to the family outing. The kids were so
excited and Doug worked long hours; she knew a day on the water would
be some well-appreciated family time. He slowly backed out of the tight

dock spot, quietly cursing the slip location. Then he pushed the throttle forward and they began to motor out of the canal to the main water of the bay. It was a small body of water with many low spots, so it was a safe place to take a family. The only area that required a bit more care was at the inlet, an opening at the east side of the bay where bigger boats and serious fishermen could access the ocean.

"Not many boats out today," Doug thought. "That'll keep the wake minimal." He glanced away from the water for a moment and watched his family with a deep appreciation. He had been an only child and enjoyed watching the interaction between Jack and Sara. Maybe it was time to add to their number. He'd bring it up to Ella after dinner tonight.

"There's the yacht club. Looks like a few of the members are starting to put their boats back in the water." Ella pointed out the marina across the way. They continued cruising around the Rehoboth Bay, pointing out sights and sounds that they had not seen since last season.

"Is that a Bald Eagle?" Jack looked up and pointed to the sky. It was good to be out again. By popular request, Doug drifted onto the sandbar that was near the resort area so everyone could stop and have a snack. It wasn't long before Sara wanted to climb out of the boat and play on the shoreline.

"Look, Mom, I found more shells." Sara had started digging and was able to gather quite a few with her spade.

"I want some, too!" Jack joined his sister on her quest for mussels, oyster shells, and sea glass. Ella watched the two on their adventure and she was very content with how her life had turned out. Those weekends in their small cottage near the beach with her two curious and thoughtful kids were once just a dream. The fact that she shared all of this with a husband whom she loved as much as the day they were married was a fortune that could not be measured. Studying Doug as he had closed his eyes for quick nap, she knew that there was nothing else she could ask for at this moment.

After about thirty minutes had passed, she noticed that some gray clouds had moved in. Most of the boats that had been in the area were starting to head back.

"Sara. Jack. Time to come back to the boat, we need to get moving," Ella called to her children.

"Oh, Mom. Just five more minutes. Our bucket is almost full," begged Sara.

"Okay, but then we have to go. The sky is starting to look a little mean." She kissed Doug awake and after rubbing his eyes, he stretched his long legs back into action. When the promised five minutes had expired, Ella gathered the two youngsters into the boat and made sure everything was put away.

"Wow that came up fast." Doug struggled to lower the overhead canvas top when the wind started to get under it and decided his time was better spent getting them under way. White caps began to slap against the pontoons. Ella had the children gathered to her, one under each arm, while Doug jumped out to manually push the vessel off of the sand. Once he felt some movement, he climbed back on and turned his attention to the cockpit controls. Turning the ignition key to get the boat started, he looked at the sky and noted that they had just enough time to pull off the sandbar and begin their motored drive back to the dock.

Without much warning, the wind began to gust with a strength that pulled the boat in the eastern direction. They were unintentionally headed toward the inlet that emptied into the Atlantic Ocean. With all the strength that Doug could summon, he pulled on the wheel wishing he'd have spent the extra money for more horsepower. His teeth were locked together as if his bite strength would help stay the unwanted movement to the east. Out in the open, his arms were being slapped with fat rain pellets that had begun to drop generously from the sky. His hands were cramping up from the grip he held on the wheel. If sheer will could have turned the boat around it would have been heading back to their canal at this moment.

But the storm that hit them was too strong and too fast. They continued to move toward the inlet as though the boat was a balloon being pushed by the breath of a child.

"Mommy, I'm scared!" Jack screamed as their bucket of sand treasures slid from one side of the deck to the other. Sara began crying at her father's inability to control their vessel. Even though she herself was not wearing one, Ella tightened everyone's life jacket and tried to calm her children.

"It's going to be okay. Daddy will get us home," she had to shout over the wind.

Water was now splashing up from the bay and onto their shoes. She tried to protect her small children by holding them close on her lap. The rain was stinging them all with water needles so she used her jacket as a makeshift tarp to cover their little faces. That also helped to hide from them the look of panic on Doug's face. She tried to get his attention by pointing to a stone jetty nearby. They might crash, but at least they could get on land before they were forced out to sea.

The thunder drowned out her voice and the screams of her children were mortifying because there was nothing she could do. She felt powerless watching Doug struggle at the wheel; she knew they were in serious trouble. Moving rapidly through the inlet, they would soon be in the ocean on a boat that could not handle the crush of the waves. With one last tug of force, he was able to turn the boat just in time to hit the stone jetty and stall out the motor. Ella finally felt that there might be hope to save them. As the boat took a hit on the side it began to turn over. She knew it was about to flip, so Ella grabbed the children and placed them over the other side of the rail. Without speaking, Doug knew he had to jump over after the children so he could move them away from the boat and onto the shore to safety. He looked over to his wife and with only his eyes Doug relayed a message that she immediately recognized. "I love you too," she mouthed to him.

"Mommy!" Ella could barely hear her daughter scream as none of their voices could be heard over the sounds of the storm. When she was confident that Doug had saved both of the children, Ella's world went dark.

Her next memory was of an orange life preserver being tossed her way. The rope was attached to someone on board a large, passing ship and with measured strokes they began pulling her from the sea. She was relieved to have been rescued but concerned about her family—she supposed that they were also saved and that she would meet them on shore. They'll huddle together and be thankful that only the boat was lost during the storm. She'll say to them, "Let's go home and have some hot chocolate." And everyone will have a story to tell their friends and family later.

Because of the ship's size it was not affected by the storm. There were cruise ships from the Baltimore Harbor close by apparently helping those that had been victimized by this sudden Nor'easter. There seemed to be hundreds of people on this ship who looked like they were all having such a good time. Perhaps it wasn't as bad as she first thought. Looking around she saw people dancing as though they had no care in the world. Some passengers were singing with pitch-perfect voices, songs that spoke to love and life experiences.

There were a few individuals, though, who seemed to have forgotten they were on vacation. A middle-aged woman was carrying so much luggage that she was struggling to move about the ship. Determined not to leave anything behind, she would not accept any help and frequently stopped to rearrange her bags so she could keep moving. A man in a business suit carried only a briefcase but was quite disturbed that he was not getting any cell reception. Finally someone in a long, pale-green gown appeared with a clipboard in her hand and offered her a soothing drink.

"Must be one of the stage performers," she thought. "They probably need the extra help since they picked up so many passengers from the storm waters."

"Thank you, this is refreshing. So did you rescue many people? I'm looking for the rest of my family, Doug, Sara, and Jack. Morgan's the last name. Do you have them on your list? I'm anxious to let them know that I'm okay," Ella asked the kind woman who had given her a drink.

"I'll have to check with the captain," she said, so Ella became slightly concerned.

"Maybe they would have been safer staying with me," she said to no one in particular. Running her hands across the swimsuit cover up that had been torn during her ordeal she turned to her new friend. "I'd like to freshen up a bit. Is there someplace I can go?" she asked.

"Of course, right this way." And the woman waved her arm directing Ella to the adjacent hallway.

Ella went into the restroom to wash up and saw her reflection in the mirror. "Guess it's true about seawater softening your hair." As it dried, it had become thicker and the natural auburn curls softly framed her face. The sun had given her a soft-rose blush. "Well, not bad for just being pulled from the sea." Ella liked what she saw. When Doug and the kids found her, she wanted to look her best so they wouldn't worry. She missed them already.

Her clothes were still damp and smelling like seawater, so she was led to the ship's store. She was told by the cashier to select any outfit that suited her style.

"But I don't have my purse. It was swept away in the surf."

"Don't worry about that right now." The cashier kindly led her to the clothing racks where someone was waiting to help her.

A shop attendant made a suggestion and she was very pleased. She had selected a light-blue paisley printed tunic over white leggings. She slipped on a pair of white satin shoes that hugged her feet. "Like walking on pillows," she thought. Ella was very pleased with the look. It felt stylish, comfortable, and frankly much nicer than anything she had at home.

The attendant held up a handbag in a similar shade of blue. "This would be the perfect accessory," she said as she held it against her outfit.

"At no charge?" Ella couldn't believe her luck. The tote was so deliciously soft.

"The captain said you deserve it after all you have been through."

After some consideration, she decided against it, as it was just one more thing to carry around and she had nothing to put in it anyway. "That's such a wonderful offer, but I need to focus on finding my family."

Still searching for Doug and the children, she went into the Grand Atrium, following the sound of instrumental music unlike anything she had ever heard before. There were two glowing young ladies playing electric violins. Dressed in shimmering gold and silver gowns garnished with crystals, both had long, braided hair; one was blonde, the other brunette.

"When we get home, I'm going to sign Sara up for violin lessons. I know she would love this."

Children were gathered in the corner of the atrium in a play area where a young lady in shorts and a golf shirt was keeping them amused. They sat on the ground with a large board game, laughing and rocking on their knees. As a mom, Ella appreciated the level of kindness the leader was showing and the cooperation of the children as they all spread out to welcome a new member to the congregation. But unfortunately, neither Sara nor Jack was part of the group.

Ella decided to walk around the ship in hopes of finding Doug. He must be here and he would know where the children are. Her last memory was of him grabbing the children before the boat crashed into the jetty. They must be tired and hungry just like she was, and anxious to get home. There were guides with T-shirts that said *Just Ask* so Ella approached one of them.

"I'm sorry to bother you, but I was wondering if there was a place where I could get something to eat. With luck, I'll see my family there. I'm sure they're as hungry as I am."

"Of course, Mrs. Morgan. I will take you to the restaurant. Right this way."

She was led into a softly decorated area with pastel velvet chairs at every table, glowing with pink overhead lighting, and chubby cherub sculptures were posted in every corner as if to watch over the dining room. Ella was offered a warm meal while she waited for news of her husband and children. All of her favorite foods were available. She stopped for a moment, wondering how the guide knew her name—but shrugged it off to exceptional service.

She chose a plate of lobster prepared three ways; there was a fat, buttery tail that overflowed from the shell, a side of soft lobster risotto, and it was all topped with velvety lobster bisque. This was followed by a raspberry Crème Brûlée that was flanked by two lemony cookies. "Oh, this is so crunchy and creamy in every bite," she said to know one in particular. To finish her meal, Ella ordered a coffee with Baileys. She was pleasantly full. As she got up from her table she couldn't help but notice what others were having. There was a man thoroughly delighted with his thick salmon platter and a pair of ladies gazing over a tower of little sandwiches, tea cakes, and fruit—giggling over the decision about what to eat first. The bubbles from their champagne glasses matched the sparkle in their eyes.

She walked by the captain's table where he was entertaining those who had led a life of serving others. A poster by the table highlighted those who had been selected and what they had contributed. Some were very impressive. Ella thought that was a nice gesture by the cruise line. But still, there was no sign of her family. She was beginning to worry.

Passing the indoor pool, she saw an elderly man in his church suit patiently sitting at a table. He was slowly eating an ice cream and watching the people go by. "Are you here by yourself?" Ella asked because she thought maybe he needed some company. "For now," he said. "But my Millie will be here shortly. I promised that I would wait for her." He smiled, so Ella put her hand on his and said, "Well, I hope she'll meet you soon so she can help you with that ice cream cone." They both laughed and she continued on her tour.

Ella heard about an art auction in one of the lounge areas, so she stopped in to see what it was all about. The room was dark, but when she focused her eyes on the paintings, it was disturbing. Each one was a scene from her life story. Some were of her as a young girl with her parents, followed by a portrait of her accepting a college diploma. There were paintings of her wedding day with Doug standing beside her. Even her children were portrayed as infants and then as they enjoyed subsequent birthdays. It was getting creepy to see her life reflected in these paintings. There was a burning in her chest that was starting to grow. Ella placed one hand on her forehead between her eyes and one on her solar plexus. She ran out to the hallway and grabbed another *Just Ask* guide.

"What is happening?" she screamed. "Where is my family?" The truth was beginning to settle in for Ella. She had not survived the storm. Within moments, the gowned woman who had met her when she first boarded the ship took her in her arms and said, "Welcome home Ella." It was her mother.

Together they walked down a hall of private suites. Ella was stunned at this new but very real scenario. "It's time to rest. This will all make more sense when you have been able to begin the separation process." Her hostess opened the door to a stateroom that was empty except for a desk and single bed positioned in the center of the room. There was a hazy outline on the bed that she immediately recognized.

"Sara." Ella knelt next to her and stroked her hair. As much as she wanted to be strong for her daughter, she could not contain her tears. "Where have you been? Have you seen Dad and Jack?"

"Mom. I've been here waiting for you." Sara seemed very strong at this moment. "Are you okay? Where is this place?"

"Sara, come back to us sweetheart. Jack and I miss you. Please wake up." Even though it was faint and seemed far away, Ella recognized Doug's voice. Sara was mildly distracted, but then returned her attention to her mother.

It was now clear that Sara was caught between worlds.

"I can stay with you so you are not alone," Sara offered. "Dad and Jack have each other, but you'll be here all by yourself."

Doug had lost his wife, and Jack his mother. It would be too painful for them to lose Sara as well. Making the most difficult decision of her life, she encouraged her daughter to return.

"Oh, my sweet Sara. You must go back. You know they need you. Who will make sure Jack learns how to tie his shoes or that Dad reads him a bedtime story?"

"Is this heaven? I don't want to leave you here, so will you come back home with me?" Sara began to weep as her strong façade started to crumble.

"Sara, we love you so much. Please wake up and come back to us." Again they heard the distant pleading and Sara seemed to look over Ella's shoulder following the voice. She was torn as to what path to take.

"I'm going to be okay. There are so many people here to help me. Sara, you must take a message back to Dad and Jack. Let them know I made it."

"Mom, no."

"Yes Sara, this is something I need you to do for me. It's very important. You have to tell them you saw me, that I looked well. Tell Jack that he's a fine young man and I'm very proud of him. And tell Dad that I will always love him." Ella stood up and looked away so her tears would not be evident.

"You do look pretty."

"And this is a safe and peaceful place. You go back to Dad and I will watch over you. I'll be there when you have your first date. I'll walk beside you when you marry the love of your life. When your children are born I will kiss them goodnight, and when you are ready to say goodbye I will be here for you. When it is time, I promise to be waiting for you."

"I don't know if I can do this." Sara was still torn.

"Let me help you." Ella's mother took charge seeing that Ella herself might not be strong enough. "Sara, listen to me and focus on my voice. As I dim the lights here, your light in the physical will become brighter. I'll count through colors as you return. When I get to purple, your favorite, you will be completely awake and with your daddy. Your memories of meeting your mother will gradually fade but you will never forget the love she feels for you." Ella was glad that her mother had taken over because she wasn't sure she had the concentration to complete the task.

"I love you, Mom," and with those last words Sara let go of her mother's hand.

"And I will always love you." Ella kissed her daughter on the forehead and moved toward the door to give her some breathing space.

"Close your eyes, Sara. Good. You have been walking for a long time and you are ready for some rest. You notice a small cottage ahead. This is the cottage where you will meet your father and brother. This is where you are supposed to be and it makes you happy to be so close. Can you see it?" asks her guide.

"Yes, I can. It's very nice." Sara smiled and nodded.

"It is nice," her guide confirmed. "Keep using your imagination until you see a red, glossy wagon by the gate. See how new it looks? You will be able to give your dolls a ride in it. On one side of the little house there is an orange tree; see a ripe, round orange, a juicy fruit just waiting to be picked. Now look over to the field of yellow sunflowers on the other side. They are waving in a soft breeze with their green leaves shining from the sunlight." From experience, she could tell that Sara was getting closer to home. She glanced at Ella to make sure she was also absorbing the experience. Convinced that Ella was still resolute, she continued.

"You see that you are wearing a cornflower-blue dress with white ruffles on the collar and sleeves. See how pretty you are walking up the sidewalk to the door. That door is a perfect shade of purple. There are carvings in the wood and a brass unicorn doorbell. Touch it. Press the bell so your daddy will know you've come home."

Within moments, Sara faded from view. Ella could hear some faint cheering in the background. After experiencing so many unfamiliar activities, everything finally seemed right again. She turned to the door where the gowned woman stood.

"Thank you Mom. That was so tender and beautiful." She paused. "I love that you were here for all of this, but I'm ready to go now. I need to see what's next for me."

They walked together to the upper levels of the ship. The pathways were lit with fairy lights. Up on the topmost deck, she saw the twin exhaust stacks.

"Looks just like angel wings."

"Yes, they do remind us to take flight," said her mother.

"Just one question, though. Why a cruise ship?" Ella asked.

"Well, it is always a choice. Sometimes it is based on the place and time where one leaves the physical. For example, someone who dies in a hospital might decide to transition in a garden attached to a large institutional building. If they are at home, perhaps they will find themselves in their favorite neighborhood. It would make sense that if one were to be near the water, the logical, human mind would find liberation and comfort on a luxury ship. And some simply have fond memories of their vacation, so this suits them. Just like you, many souls are finding this a safe space. It is a different and special place for everyone."

A family came aboard dripping wet and confused about their new location. Ella smiled to herself thinking that they were in for a big surprise.

She stopped to watch an outdoor movie that was playing by the café and on the big screen she saw Sara sitting up in bed being embraced by her father. Jack sat on the bedside with a toy and he looked very happy to see his sister responding to them. Ella was relieved that her mother had intervened to send Sara back to the physical world. In her heart, she knew that they would be alright and that her family would be reunited when all the lessons had been learned and the experiences had been completed. She was safe and knew that they would be, too.

Ella had looked through a catalogue when she had first arrived, and now that she had selected her shore excursion she was lighter and felt free to move on at her own pace. With confidence in her journey Ella floated from the confines of the ship, spreading her wings, ready for her next adventure.

INTERVIEW WITH
AN ASTRAL GUIDE

"Carter! Get in here!" growled the executive editor for the Astral City News Network. Carter jumped out of his chair and quickly walked toward the glass office in the front of the cubicle farm. The journalists worked at cheap, undersized desks and rarely spoke to anyone in the office. Because they were given assignments to create local Astral City news, human interest stories, and new arrival and departure updates, it was a repetitive and predictable environment. Carter was just trying to put in his time until he could break a big story, something important.

"Yes sir?" he said meekly, anxious about what his next project would be.

"You've been reassigned. You are off the daily desk, and moving upstairs. Get your things and go, they're waiting for you." The editor briefly looked up to relay the message. Carter could barely contain his excitement. All of the boring stories created by this department had worn him down over the years. He was finally moving on.

Carter gathered his few belongings and headed toward the elevator. None of his co-workers even reacted to his departure. They were too busy developing new angles to the same old stories. When the door closed and the elevator began to move upward he was elated. Now he would finally share news that would help people. No more creating fluff stories, those boring articles about current Astral City events.

Up on the seventh floor, there were just a few empty desks available so Carter picked the one nearest the window. Easing into a soft, leather chair he was warmed by the streaming light coming through the tall, glass panes. There was soft music playing through invisible speakers, and thick carpet under his feet. "There must be a bigger budget in this department," he thought to himself.

"Welcome. Call me Myra. I am very glad to have you here with us." His new editor had just arrived. Carter noticed her striking features—long white hair tied back in a complicated two-part braid, deep-set eyes peering out from flawless brown skin. After his last assignment, the gentle tone of her voice was unexpected. "Do you have an objective in mind?"

"Well, yes. I am looking forward to a real and meaningful assignment." Carter stood as a sign of respect for his new supervisor.

"Can you be more specific?" Myra asked, waving her hand encouraging him to take his seat as she took the chair opposite him. Leaning forward, she sat with her elbows perched on his desk trying to assess his competence for this job.

"I would like to interview a being from beyond our heaven, one with greater knowledge who can share insights into the nature of our reality, teach us how to live with confidence and purpose."

"Sounds ambitious," Myra said as she looked directly into his eyes. "And you think you're up for it?"

"I know people are hungry for substance." Carter sounded sure about this.

"So more truth, less theater?"

"Exactly," said Carter, relieved that she seemed to understand just what he was looking for. "And I know I'm the one to do it. I'm ready."

A hint of a smile appeared on her face. "I believe that you are. If there is anything I can get for you, just give me a thought and I'll make it happen." Her dress rustled softly as she rose from her seat and floated away leaving only a small note that said, "Interview at midnight in the library." He discovered that the building had a research library on the top floor; his first assignment was to meet someone named Arden.

Carter was thrilled that Myra had sent him to cover this big story. It had never been done before, at least not in his five years of reporting the news. Interviewing an astral guide was a real breakthrough. Entering the library he was anxious as he surveyed the walls of books that surrounded him. Endless rows with volumes of information. It was all there, but did anyone see it? Without warning, Carter heard a voice that came from beyond the dusty shelves.

"All of us are multidimensional beings; we exist in many dimensions at this moment. The path to self-knowledge and liberation from the illusions of form is within us." Arden approached the young man in a single fluid movement. His presence emanated an ethereal glow that highlighted his short white hair and clean-shaven appearance.

"Hello, my name is Carter. I'm from the Astral City News Network." He held out his hand to introduce himself. "I'd like to thank you very much for agreeing to this interview. To have an exclusive insight into your world is an honor I will not forget,"

Arden smiled as he took Carter's hand. "The honor is mine. For too long we have tried to send subtle messages to the astral inhabitants as they navigate their realities. But they often brush off our messages as a dream or coincidence. Apparently subtle contact is inefficient; we hope a direct approach will prove more effective."

They took a seat across from each other on armless, white, highback chairs. Between them was a round, translucent table with pens and notebooks. Arden sat comfortably, while Carter nervously examined his notes. He was an old-school reporter who wanted to back up the recordings with handwritten notes, allowing him to better absorb the energy of the interview.

"So let's get to it. What is the most important message I can give to the Astral City residents?" asked Carter.

After a moment Arden calmly responded, "The inhabitants remain fixated on the outer appearance of their reality instead of focusing on the inner essence."

"What do you mean? Can you explain that?"

"Most astral inhabitants continue to cling to the beliefs and limits they learned while on Earth; they still pursue deity worship and rituals instead of self-exploration and self-knowledge. They maintain the same physical self-image they wore during their last Earth visit. Indoctrinated mindsets are reluctant to change." Arden paused so that Carter could catch up on his notes. "Souls create their own version of heaven or hell based upon their thoughts."

"But Astral City residents love our beautiful city; they feel blessed to live here. We consider this to be heaven," Carter immediately responded in defense of his world.

"Yes, the inhabitants think they are in heaven; instead they are trapped in a self-created gilded cage." As he spoke Arden studied Carter's facial expressions. "They remain unaware of their true self, their multidimensional nature, and the countless opportunities for growth available to them. They have blindly accepted the first reality they experienced when they shed their physical bodies."

Carter was visibly disturbed by the thought of a gilded cage and responded sharply to his guest. "My readers would find that hard to accept. We feel free. There's no aging, disease, wars, or any of the hellish crap we experienced on Earth. This is a perfect heaven to us."

"You are correct; compared to Earth it is. However, it's a reality with serious inherent limits. Your city is molded by the inhabitants' collective mindset, a direct result of their many life experiences in the physical. For example, they still believe they are bipedal humanoids. They remain attached to density, continuing to see their surroundings within a physical frame of reference. They remain unaware of what they are, where they are headed, and their purpose for existence." Arden stood and began to walk away from the table.

Carter considered Arden's last comment. "That's an alarming thought; this is not the interview I envisioned at all."

Arden turned and smiled, for he knew he was getting some reaction from the young man. "That is the point of our conversation is it not? A more expansive vision is essential for the evolution of consciousness to occur. Change is challenging."

"But, this defies our entire perception of heaven! You are saying that millions—maybe billions—of us are not in a real heaven at all. We are living in a prison compound limited by our own thoughts and beliefs." Carter was trying to develop a storyline here that he could present to his editor, but it was beginning to look doubtful.

"Don't misunderstand the point. Your current reality is pleasant. But it is also a pale reflection of its potential."

Arden stood next to his seat and waited for Carter to look up from his notes.

"Ask yourself, can you fly or move through walls? Have you ever traveled to another reality beyond the perimeter of Astral City?" Arden watched as Carter shook his head in the negative.

"Why not? Soul has no limits!" As Arden continued to speak he gently rose, hovering several feet from the ground. "There is no gravity in this reality; why can't the Astral City residents float or fly on command?"

"I've always assumed that our limits are a natural part of living in heaven. We all have the same basic capabilities, so it seems normal."

Arden slowly descended as he spoke, "The flawed beliefs of the inhabitants have created those limits. Come, take my hand."

Carter rose from his seat and grasped his hand. They both gently lifted several feet off of the carpet.

"This is amazing!" Carter was wobbling as he tried to gain his balance while floating in mid-air.

"All nonphysical realities are thought-responsive to some degree, molded by the collective mindset of the inhabitants. This creates a comfortable heaven but one limited by the group-consensus thoughts." As they slowly returned to the stability of the floor Carter felt himself begin to breathe again.

"I don't know if my editor will even publish this. It's radical, totally counter to our way of thinking." Carter said this as much to himself as he did to Arden.

"The truth is outrageous to many. The deception of humanity continues even after transition from the physical because the inhabitants continue to believe the indoctrination so prevalent on Earth. They become content in their concept of heaven and feel no need to seek the truth of their existence beyond their new reality. They fail to explore inward to the Source." Arden never tired of seeing the beauty of the night sky, so he stood and walked toward a floor-to-ceiling window.

"Inward? I don't understand the concept? Why is 'inward' so important?" Carter joined him but left his notebook behind on the table.

"Because inward is the universal path; this is where the answers reside." Arden held his hand in the center of his chest. "Ask yourself, what are you, why are you here, where are you going, what's the purpose? Even after the physical incarnation is complete, souls in human form settle for primitive beliefs and fail to seek the answers for themselves." Carter's eyes had begun to glaze over. Arden knew he would have to show him exactly what he meant.

"Inward is a difficult concept for many. Place your hand on my arm." Arden extended his right arm toward the skeptic.

The moment Carter took his arm there was an intense sense of inner motion as the world around him appeared to dissolve away. In an instant he was in a bright new reality, an environment formless yet radiating a peaceful, soft, white light. Disoriented by the rapid change, he began to realize that he possessed no body at all. He was 360 degrees of perception without form. Carter was terrified and exhilarated at the same time by this radical transformation.

"Incredible, I can see everything, in all directions. Where am I? What am I?"

"You have moved inward within yourself. This is your true self and your natural perception as soul."

"I feel so light and free—empowered. Now I see what you mean—we are not our bodies."

"We are pure consciousness with the creative ability to operate any external form for our expression and experience. We are magnificent beings who have yet to realize our unlimited potential. All of the countless manifestations of form are but temporary tools—vehicles of soul. Please emphasize to your readers that we are not three-dimensional humanoids."

"Then why is the physical world important? Why do we even need it?"

"Physical realities change quickly; this makes way for the new. How do we learn if we keep returning to the same classroom? The greater the challenge, the more profound the lesson and the deeper the knowledge obtained. In many ways the physical is the ultimate reality simulation for soul."

"Is entering the physical mandatory?" Even now, Carter was considering whether—given a choice—he would ever want to return to Earth, knowing what Arden just described.

"Not at all, it's a personal decision. Billions of souls have never experienced the physical, nor do they ever plan to. Many consider the physical a far too intense and arduous environment."

"So then, why is physical life so hard for so many? Why can't we all just be happy and have fun experiences?"

"It is a pleasant thought, but what do you learn from an easy life? On Earth a soul's education involves intense learning through personal challenges and the opportunity to experience inner growth and knowledge. Evolution of consciousness is never stagnant. Pain and pleasure are fleeting moments in the eternity of soul."

"That makes sense, but it isn't the answer most of us look for."

"Grasping the awesome reality of our immortality is difficult for those attached to the limits of form. We are unique beings, each traveling our own path—sometimes smooth, sometimes rocky; the specifics of your journey are up to you."

"So you are saying that we can all choose our own path?" Carter asked.

"Of course—free will dominates the evolutionary cycle. Each soul orchestrates its own educational agenda, repeating the personal lessons until they are absorbed."

"Now that you've told me about the limitations in my environment, are there other heavens?" Carter was somewhat curious about the universe, but had never really thought about the potential of other worlds.

"There are more realities than grains of sand on the beach, and each is the direct result of the collective thoughts of the inhabitants."

"Are all these heavens human?" As a journalist, Carter had always been interested in other life forms but had not had any direct experience with a non-human entity.

"The human species is but one of the countless vehicles for soul to select. Each environment and timeline offers specific qualities and educational opportunities. The human experience provides an effective choice for spiritual development; however, humans have proven to be herd animals. Their need to conform to the collective reality creates serious challenges to their spiritual evolution."

They slowly returned to the research library in the Astral City reality. Carter's excitement was still running high. "Now I am beginning to understand. Thank you for this experience, it is life changing!" Carter took a moment to adjust to the feeling of a body once again. As he shook his arms and bent his legs to reassure himself that they were still functional, he continued to talk through what he had just experienced. "I will need some time to ponder all this. These concepts are going way beyond what I thought the interview would produce. Expressing this information to my readers will be a serious challenge."

"I do have a few more questions though," Carter said as he returned to his notes. "How many guides exist and what is their primary function?"

"The dimensions are vast and extremely busy, populated by countless realities and trillions of souls. There exists a wide range of guides and helpers with specific areas of expertise. For example, some guides focus on dream-weaving; others are multidimensional trainers who teach the skills of inner exploration. Some specialize in the needs of children. Many assist the transition of souls during their exit from the physical and entry into the astral worlds."

"You mean death?"

"We don't use that word. The end of the physical body life is simply the continuation of a spiritual journey."

"Do souls always incarnate as humans from life to life?" Carter asked.

"Most souls become comfortable with a single species and use it through multiple incarnations."

"What is the purpose for this entire process? It seems so slow and repetitive."

"The purpose is the evolution of soul through individual experiences. We learn by being, by experiencing what we choose to know. The educational system is brilliantly conceived: each soul creates its individual learning agenda within the different realities and dimensions. Since we are immortal the time this takes is irrelevant." Arden ran his hand over the books on a nearby shelf. He looked appreciatively at all the learning that had taken place so far in this reality.

"I can't thank you enough. I am so inspired. Do you have any final words for my readers?" Carter knew it was time to wrap this up.

"Remember we exist beyond form, beyond the constraints of time and space. You are a powerful creative being with the ability to obtain the answers to all of life's mysteries. Be completely open-minded and embrace your life lessons, especially when they are uncomfortable and stretch you beyond your comfort zone."

Arden stopped for a moment to emphasize his final statement. "To truly know the answers to the mysteries of our existence it's essential to go beyond all beliefs and become an active spiritual explorer."

"This has been an amazing night. I truly appreciate your time. We can go out this way." He was offering Arden an escort to the door, but it wasn't necessary as he was already gone when Carter looked up from his notepad.

"I need to tell my coworkers about this." His first thought was to go back and visit his previous office. If they knew about this they would stop wasting energy chasing superficial stories. As he approached the elevator to return to his former office, Myra joined him.

"Don't bother. They are not in a place where they will hear what you have to say. Remember Arden told you that everyone is on their own path. He came to you when you were ready to accept new ideas, challenging the established reality construct. Not everyone will understand this knowledge." Myra left the elevator lobby as quietly as she had arrived.

After his time with Arden, Carter felt at peace, content in how far he had come in his spiritual journey in just one night. Now he had a story to write, one that would be transformational. The reality of heaven will be mind-expanding for those who are ready for the truth. And for those on a different path, well, the knowledge would be there when they became ready for it.

THE TEACHER BECOMES
THE STUDENT

Laura Wheaton loved children. Especially at this age, they were so innocent, so trusting. They were curious about everything and their whole lives were in front of them. Such possibilities lie ahead. She often felt that way about her own life as well. That's why her vocation suited her. In her favorite position, sitting at the front of her classroom, she had just finished reading a story to her tiny audience. This one was about a puppy that was just a little pokey.

Behind the story-telling area was the learning center. The chairs and desks were very low to the ground to accommodate the students' short legs, and were painted in bright colors. There was a bookcase running the length of one wall in the same color pattern of sea blue, cherry red, and grass green. Books and games filled the shelves, making this a fun place to learn. Laura had positioned the chalk boards and activity centers so that the children could easily reach them. It sometimes made her feel like a giant in a room of little humans.

After story time, the children began to play in groups of three and four. Today she noticed that one of the children, a little girl, sat in the corner by herself. She wiped a single tear from her cheek, so Laura moved over to where she was and knelt beside her.

"What's wrong, Ashley?" Laura gently asked the little girl.

"My great-grandma died. I miss my Nana."

"Oh I am so sorry to hear about that. But don't be too sad, your Nana is in a wonderful place."

"How do you know that?" Ashley asked through her little-girl sobs.

Laura wiped away the little girl's tears. Laura lovingly touched a locket around her neck, and then opened it to reveal a picture of her Aunt Matilda.

"This is a picture of my aunt. She's in heaven now and I miss her, just like you miss your great-grandmother. But I know she's very happy where she is."

"Are you sure?"

"Oh yes, I dream about her. She's planting flowers in her garden. I can almost hear her humming."

"Maybe my Nana will be playing the piano. She used to teach little kids like me." Ashley began to feel better.

"I'll bet she is." Laura gave the little girl a hug.

Andy, her fiancé, was there to pick Laura up for their Friday date night. He watched the scene from the doorway, always moved by the way Laura could comfort a child. A little boy spotted him and began to snicker. Within seconds, the entire class was pointing in Andy's direction and giggling. Laura looked up and smiled. The bell rang and she moved into action, rounding up the little ones and getting their belongings together.

"Okay, everyone, let's get our backpacks, jackets, and lunch boxes. Good. Now line up at the door."

The class erupted into a flurry of activity as they gathered their belongings. The room was filled with the tapping of little shoes on the floor, the snapping of their bags off of their hooks, and the sound of lunch-boxes scraping the shelves as they were grabbed by their little owners.

These were the sounds that Laura loved. Like miniature soldiers in comical clothing, the group lined up by the door as directed. Andy stepped aside and watched them file by on their way to the bus. One by one, they looked up at him and smiled.

A chorus of twenty goodbyes was heard as the children were led out of the room by the teacher's helper. Andy grinned at Laura as the line of children marched past him. When the last child left, Laura leaned in close to him and breathed in his fragrance. She loved the way his skin smelled; he wore no aftershave—it was just his natural scent that made her fall a little more in love with him every day.

"I'm starving. Where are you taking me to dinner? Another pizza from Grotto's?" she asked as she pulled back, not letting go of his hands.

"No—even though they have a way with cheese and sauce that is unparalleled in the modern world," he said as he brushed his lips against her right hand. "Tonight I have planned something special. I know the perfect place where the menu is quite simple and the view is magnificent."

Moonlight illuminated the dry-docked boat that had been Andy's project for the last few months. They sat at the highest peak of the cabin overlooking the marina with a spectacular view of the harbor. The lights strung over the dock slips cast shimmering, ghostlike images and the faint sound of a harbor bell echoed across the water. The atmosphere was seductively romantic.

"God, I love being here and being with you." Andy looked in Laura's deep brown eyes, thinking about how perfect the setting was.

"It's breathtaking. Like Christmas all year long," said Laura referring to the lights below.

Andy reached into an old paint bucket and pulled out a bottle of chilled wine. He filled Laura's glass and proposed a toast.

"To us."

"Forever."

Their glasses touched. Andy stood and held her hands, gently pulling her up. With eyes wide open, he lifted her chin with his bent forefinger and gently brushed her lips with his. Embracing her with a desire that their bodies would melt into one, he led her in a slow dance along the moon-swept deck. In silence, they were gliding along the length of the boat with the evening light casting graceful shadows across the deck.

"This is so nice, dinner and dancing. Andy, you do know how to make a girl feel special. I want to spend the rest of my life trying to do the same for you," said Laura, and she meant every word. Never had she felt so happy.

The next morning they left the cabin laughing and outlining their plan for the day. Holding hands, they walked to Andy's motorcycle and headed out of the marina lot. Time seemed to slow as Andy leisurely moved through traffic. The first signs of morning were everywhere. Shopkeepers were opening their doors, morning joggers were out trying to beat the car traffic, and a few of the town locals were having coffee at a park bench. The morning air was a little chilly, so Laura hugged him tight as they flowed through the quaint streets of historic Long Neck Harbor. It was almost time to put the bike away for the winter, so he was pleased that they could have such a clear day for the last ride of the season.

He found a parking space near the toy shop where Laura would be looking for small prizes for her students. She linked her arm under his while they looked through the holiday exhibits that were set up in almost every shop window. At the *Tick-Tock Clock Shop* Laura made a mental note of Andy's interest in an antique pocket watch housed in an ornately carved box. That would make a perfect wedding gift for him. She thought about even having it engraved for a more personal touch.

They moved on past the *Sweet Shop* forgoing the temptation provided by the many flavors of homemade fudge displayed in the shop window and headed to the store that displayed educational toys. This is where she would be spending some time this morning as she always liked to encourage her students to use their minds through creative endeavors. As she opened the door, a young child ran past her laughing and saying, "Come and get me!" to her exasperated mother. "Ava, come back here. Take my hand!"

Laura's instincts kicked in and she turned to grab the child who had moved too quickly for her mother. She knew she had to catch her before she went out into the street. Just a few steps away from the door and Laura was able to grab the girl and put her back into the arms of her mother. With an unnatural silence a car had rounded the corner, the driver not noticing the woman who remained on the street side of the curb.

"Laura, watch out!" Andy was too late with his warning and could not reach her in time to stop what was about to happen.

The force of the impact was so strong that it threw Laura forward. Her body struck the hood of the car and then slammed into the windshield. The offending driver stopped with a jerk as Laura's wounded body slid off the hood and hit the ground. Tires screamed as the big sedan wrenched into reverse and then fishtailed out of sight.

Andy jumped the curb and fell to his knees trying to protect Laura's battered body as she lay motionless by the side of the road. He touched her hands, stroked her face, and cried her name out loud trying to get a response from her. Pulling her face toward him, he spoke with a rare panic in his voice.

"Laura . . . God, Laura . . ." Andy was totally focused on her, unaware of anything else happening around them. In shock, he rolled her limp body into his lap, desperately trying to revive her. His shaking hands attempted to stop her bleeding, but to no avail. Slowly, her eyes fluttered and she managed to move her lips slightly.

"Andy, I . . . love, forever . . ." Her words ended with a barely discernible gasp.

"Laura, no! I need you, hold on!" Andy was screaming now. Loudly sobbing, he held her tightly and rocked her limp body. "Please, God, no . . . please!"

A crowd of curious onlookers was beginning to gather around them. He clutched her quiet body in his arms and gently kissed her lips trying to breathe life into her. Although Andy and the crowd did not see it, Laura's spirit was exiting her body. In her misty form, she stood next him, trying to understand what had just happened. She was still a little foggy as she tried to manage her mixed emotions—relief at what she thought was her survival, but sadness for Andy at the same time. She wasn't sure why, but he was devastated. He held a lifeless body in his lap. For a moment, time ceased to exist as she tried to grasp reality. The body his tears were falling on was hers.

"No, no, no. Laura. Somebody help me!"

Sirens were heard in the background, at first from a distance, but then louder and louder as they approached the crash site. A few people were vainly attempting to help but most were just staring in horror, as they had never witnessed anything like the deadly scene in front of them.

"No, no. This can't be happening." Andy could barely choke the words out of his closed throat.

Gradually there emerged a glowing spirit—gliding, almost floating—toward the scene. It was Laura's aunt, Matilda Buckner. She was trim woman in her late sixties, her face twisted with the pain of seeing her beautiful niece seemingly taken from her earthly life. Dressed in a rainbow-striped sweater over leopard-skin leggings, her silver-blue hair was covered by a gold turban. There was a shining aura around her that became more prominent as she got closer to the beautiful young woman whom she had raised from a girl. With ease, Matilda stepped through several of the onlookers to get to her. She looked down at the carnage and shook her head.

"Oh, sweetie, I am so sorry," said a gentle female voice.

"What just happened?" Laura asked her question to no one in particular.

Laura turned and looked toward the voice that had just addressed her. She stared in disbelief for a moment. "Auntie? What are you doing here? I thought you were . . ." Although Laura was hesitant to admit the facts of her current situation, she still felt the need to verify it.

"Yes dear, that's right, for a few years now. You remember? Ah, what a peaceful sleep it was." She seemed to get a bit lost in the memory. "But more importantly, how do I look now?" She asked the question as much to change the subject for herself as for Laura. Matilda smiled and smoothed her sweater around her slim hips.

"If you're here, does that mean I'm . . ." She looked tearfully again at her bleeding, broken body in Andy's arms. She suddenly felt overwhelmingly sad, realizing that she might not be in control anymore.

"It seems like it might be your time. A little earlier than I'd thought, but we don't get to see the calendar even up there," she said and pointed to the sky.

Laura and Matilda watched helplessly as the scene progressed. An emergency medical technician jumped from the cab of his ambulance and rushed over to check Laura's life signs. He shook his head and moved his hand from her neck.

"Do CPR or something! Don't give up. You can bring her back. Help her, don't give up," he begged the man in uniform. Andy was choking; his throat was closing as his emotional pain was far greater than anything he had ever felt before. Still in shock, Andy refused to release her body. He held her tightly, trying to squeeze his own life into hers.

"Sir, let us do our job. We'll move her into the van so you can both be more comfortable." He gently pried Andy's hands from Laura's still-warm but motionless body.

Laura was gently lifted from Andy's arms and placed on a stretcher that rolled into the ambulance. Andy insisted on riding with her body, as if to deny that the accident had happened. As a concession to the grieving man, they did not cover her face with a sheet, but allowed him to extend his goodbye to her.

Laura's etheric gaze was transfixed on the sights in front of her. She felt frozen, incapable to change the situation. Andy continued to stroke the top of Laura's hand while her spiritual form watched from several feet away. She turned to her aunt.

"But we were getting married. As soon as the boat was painted, Andy was going to put it into the water. A ship captain was scheduled to conduct the ceremony. We were going to honeymoon around the bay. It was all planned. I have to go back to him. I'm not ready to leave."

"I know, dear. I'm sure you don't think you're ready, but we can't always choose when it's time to go." Matilda took Laura's hand, holding it warmly. She tried to console her.

"No, it doesn't feel right. Please, can't you help me?" Laura was pleading.

"I wish I could help you child. But I don't have that kind of power. All I know is that if it is your time to pass . . . well, then I'm here to help you make the crossing." Matilda knew she had to act quickly, so in a dramatic gesture, she took Laura by the hand and waved her other hand toward the sky. "It's time to go. Today is the day that you move closer to God."

What happened next was the most beautiful thing that Laura had ever seen. Swirling stars and mist surrounded them. There were pinpoints of light in a twisting river of vibrant color. There were the purest gold streams and crystal-clear blue flurries, greens so fresh you could almost smell them, and the warm, caressing tones of red and orange. They mixed perfectly, forming a gentle rainbow blanket of splendor. Laura felt safe; her sadness began to fade.

As the colors became paler, she was reminded of an Easter parade with all the soft watery pinks, blues, and yellows of a new spring day. Gradually, all color had faded and she was wrapped in pure, white warmth. The glow lifted her effortlessly with her aunt beside her and as they left the Earth a flash of light signaled their exit, a flash that no one else witnessed.

A Bermuda-style, two-story cottage with a wide porch came into her focus. The pink stucco reminded Laura of fresh bubble gum. Sunny-yellow shutters surrounded the four symmetrical windows. Laura and her aunt walked along a beautiful flower border that led to the house. Matilda's clothing had changed during the journey. Laura marveled at the bright flowered coveralls and crisp, yellow blouse. She watched as her aunt adjusted the brim of the wide straw hat that shaded her from the sun. Laura, on the hand, was still wearing her jeans and Long Neck Harbor sweatshirt from the accident, but thankfully the bloodstains had disappeared.

"Ah, it feels good to be home." Matilda stepped up onto the porch and plopped herself down onto a swinging bench. She knew she had to give Laura some time to adjust.

"This looks like your house when I was a little girl, Aunt Matilda." Laura looked around in wonder. She ran her hand across the porch railing as if to make sure it was real.

"I always was comfortable here, why change a good thing? And now that you're here, call me Tilly. Everyone does." Tilly directed Laura's attention to a magnificent garden where there were endless varieties of exotic, blooming flowers in colors that Laura had never seen before. At the front was a simple plaque that read *Tilly's Garden.*

"I'm still planting and tending to my blossoms. Only here, it's a little easier." Tilly waved her hand over a large patch of yellow tulips and they immediately changed to a brilliant red. Laura was impressed.

"I knew you would be busy in the garden. But I don't understand. You only have to wave your hand?"

"No, it's really all up here. I just like to be dramatic" Tilly pointed to her head and laughed.

"Where are we? What is this place?" Laura asked.

"Some people call it heaven but I just call it home." Tilly was trying to simplify the concepts for Laura. She knew it would be quite some time before Laura would fully understand where she was. Next, she appraised the clothes of her young niece.

"Now, let's do something about your wardrobe. How about this?" and Laura was instantly dressed in the identical outfit as Tilly. She looked down at the bright colors and shook her head.

"I don't think so, Tilly. This just isn't me."

"Then you pick something. Just focus on what you like. But be specific." Tilly pointed both hands to her temples to emphasize the statement.

Laura looked down and concentrated, but nothing happened. She squeezed her eyes shut and really tried to focus.

"Sundress. Pink." Her hands clenched with nervous energy, Laura spoke her wish out loud. But still her clothes had not changed.

"Dear, don't think so hard about it, just know it. Say 'I am wearing a pink sundress' and then picture it in your mind as being so."

"Okay. I am wearing a pink sundress." This time her eyes were wide open and within a second, her thought became a reality. A short-sleeved, pale-pink cotton dress with delicate embroidery on the bodice appeared and she beamed with satisfaction. "Now this is more like it."

"Well, if you ask me, it's a little boring, but it's your thing."

Still amazed, Laura touched the dress.

"Aunt Matilda, I have so many questions."

"No more Aunt Matilda! It's Tilly. And there's plenty of time for that. For now, you should get some rest. I redecorated your old room. I hope you like it. But if you don't . . ."

"I know, just change it."

"Well, I think you're catching on." Tilly gave her a warm hug and a kiss on the forehead.

Following her direction Laura walked up the stairs to the bedroom that had been prepared for her. Opening the door, her eyes were immediately drawn to a mural painted on the wall. There was a painful tightness in her chest as she recognized a scene from her classroom. Andy was waiting in the back of the room for her while she finished singing a song with her students. When he joined in for the chorus, the whole class started laughing at his terrible tone. She ran her trembling hand over the picture. Everything changes.

After some rest, Laura left her room and found a cozy rocking chair on the front porch. She was comfortable but still depressed, deep in thought. Tilly came out the front door absolutely overflowing with energy.

"Good morning! Feeling better?"

"Yes. But I don't understand how I can be so happy and in love one minute and the next, everything is lost."

"Ahhh, emotions. Those pesky feelings—happy then sad, frustrated and then grateful. We can be playful one minute and serious the next. They always seem to come in pairs. You see, in order to experience the very fullest extent of one, you must know what the other side of it feels like. The world would be unbalanced if only one side of the story were told. So, to feel the deepest love, you must know the most painful loss."

"I'm not sure that I understand." Laura shrugged her shoulders.

"Okay, think of it like this. If you never felt the bleakest, damp, cold, winter day, how would you ever truly appreciate the beautiful warmth of summer?"

"I think I'm beginning to see. The only reason I feel such sadness is because I have experienced a rich happiness?"

"I think you've got the basics." Tilly brushed Laura's hair away from her face and chucked her on the chin.

"Enough of the gloomies. Get ready to have some fun! Come on, let's do something!" Tilly said as she jumped up from her chair and struck a pose. When she saw a little hint of a smile from Laura she dance-stepped over toward her.

Tilly took her hands and they disappeared in a flash of light. Laura thought that this mode of travel—while convenient—was also breathtakingly sudden. In the next moment Tilly was driving her classic gleaming white, Cadillac convertible through a shopping area parking lot with Laura at her side. She easily found an open parking space right by the entrance. Laura was amused by this mode of transportation.

"What's with the car?" Laura asked

"That's the fun of it. I don't need it, I just like it. Now let's go shopping." Tilly and Laura seemed to glide along toward the sparkling building.

As she glanced up at the multi-colored iridescent sign that welcomed them to *Paradise Shopping Village*, Laura was again shocked by the rapid movement and appearance of her new landscape. She didn't think she'd ever be shopping in a mall again, just like so many other things that had happened lately that she did not expect. But Tilly knew that nothing could cheer a girl up like a day of retail therapy.

"First stop, some clothes to perk up your wardrobe." Tilly approached the entrance and two handsome men in tuxedos held the crystal doors wide open for the two guests. Tilly acknowledged them with a smile and slight nod of her head.

"But, I thought . . ." Laura had to walk quickly to keep up with her aunt. She directed Laura to a clothing store named *Everything Fits*.

"Yes, you can just think of any designer dress and it will appear. What is it you young girls are wearing now? Come on sweetie, let's take a look around. I could sure use a new poncho. See anything that you like?" Tilly winked at Laura and began to walk toward a rack of the knit ponchos she was looking for. As she began to push hangers aside to inspect the color selection, she looked toward Laura, who had found a display of fun T-shirts that had caught her interest.

"Nothing has a size marked on it." Laura looked through the wide-ranging selection.

"Just pick one, dearie. I'm sure it will look spectacular!" Tilly encouraged her student. And to Laura's delight everything did fit her perfectly. Tilly emerged from the dressing room wearing an especially outrageous outfit. It had pink feathers hanging from the sleeves, and sparkling gems stitched around the neckline.

"Am I a princess? Or an angel?" Tilly twirled around the floor in her creation.

They looked at each other and laughed, assuring that the selection was just perfect. For a moment, Laura wondered how they would pay for their purchases, but surprisingly—when they reached the door—no payment was required.

They bustled by some other shoppers into a store named *Just For You*. As Laura looked at various items, she saw luggage, sweatshirts, picture frames, and more; she was impressed that every item she picked up was personalized with her name or initials. Her only regret was that Andy's last name would not be on her monogramed things. She selected some linen and exited the store with a polite smile and wave to the cashier. That was the only payment required.

"This is fun, Tilly," she said as she walked past an art exhibit to the up escalator. She smiled to herself at the metaphor.

"Okay, where next? Your choice," Tilly said, wanting Laura to lead the way.

"Let's get something to eat. What would be the least crowded? I don't want to wait in line."

"Sweetie, it's your choice. And there are no lines here." Tilly knew it would take some time before Laura fully understood.

They found a small café named *Escapes* and went inside. As Laura took in the sights and sounds of the place, she stared in awe. A narrow hallway opened to a magnificent rain forest that extended to the horizon. The sounds of wild birds were lyrical as a hostess led them along a garden path to a table surrounded by exotic, colorful flowers, the columns draped in deep-green vines. To the right was a panoramic vision of Victoria Falls.

"This is wild. How did you find this place?" Laura asked, but before she allowed Tilly to respond, she answered her own question. "I know. I created this with my thoughts because I wanted to get away to somewhere that I had never been before."

"Yes, you create what you need. Our thoughts manifest our reality. You're beginning to understand." Tilly couldn't help feeling a little bit proud of Laura's progress.

Wishing to take a walk after eating, Laura found herself in a peaceful park area. By a children's playground she sat on a bench, lost in the thoughts of her previous life. Tilly materialized near the park's fountain and started to step toward her, but she remained silent, instinctively knowing that her niece needed some quiet time. Laura was thinking about her mother and how she had been taken from her at such an early age. In all the lessons that Tilly had been providing, this was one that she couldn't grasp.

"I don't understand why my mom had to die at such a young age. I needed her so much and she wasn't there for me."

"No one can explain another person's path, Laura. Her journey wasn't about you and what you wanted. It was about her and the lessons she needed to progress to the next level. You are simply, let's just say, an accessory."

"Oh." Laura sounded disappointed.

Lucky for Laura, her aunt was always there for her. She had taken the young girl to her home several weeks after her mother passed. Laura didn't see her father again until years later. When her mother died, her father wasn't equipped to handle raising a young girl. The drugs he relied on to get him through each painful day weakened his system and eventually took his life. After years of being both mother and father, Tilly had successfully raised Laura to adulthood. The day Laura graduated from university she drove Tilly home and then went to her friend's house for a graduation party.

Later that evening, Matilda Buckner, knowing that she had completed her task of keeping Laura safe, lay down to sleep. Her heart, which had never truly healed from losing her sister, finally gave out. Laura, who barely remembered her own parents, was devastated that she had lost the only mother she had ever really known.

"Why didn't my mom or dad meet me here? Where are they?"

"Your mom came to heaven many years ago." Tilly stroked Laura's hair. "I remember she was here when I passed. It was important for her to meet me, to thank me for raising you," she continued. Tilly stood and walked a few steps away. She looked out as if she were picturing the event.

"Like a chain, we are met by those who were most important to us. By that I mean the most significant relationships." Tilly resumed her explanation after a few moments of thought.

"So, where is she now?" asked Laura.

"Your mother has moved on. God has other plans for her. She knew that—as in life—I would take care of you in death. So she felt it was time for her next role."

"And my . . . dad?" Laura wasn't comfortable using that expression.

"He has much to learn before he arrives at this place. Let's just leave it at that."

"Oh." She didn't understand, but wasn't really concerned about it either.

"I hope you aren't too disappointed, dear."

"No, just the opposite. You have been the best guide I could ask for. Just curious, that's all." She hoped she hadn't hurt her feelings.

"I'm sorry. I should have explained that to you sooner," Tilly said. "So what else is on your mind?"

"I'm a little blue."

"Dear, it's natural to feel a bit down now and then, but it's important for you to know that your thoughts create what you experience."

"What do you mean?" Laura looked up at her heavenly mentor.

"Our thoughts are much more powerful than most people know. The substance here is less dense than matter, so it can be altered quickly with a focused thought."

"Like the tulips?" asked Laura.

"Yes, exactly like the tulips. Even your ability to move around is determined by thought. If you want to visit someone, just picture their face in your mind. It's easy. Try it." Tilly challenged her.

Laura closed her eyes and disappeared. There was a sensation of incredible speed. Suddenly she was standing at the scene of the accident looking at Andy as he wept, watching his intense grief as her body was being moved into the back of the ambulance. Overwhelmed, Laura snapped back to Tilly's side, shaken and out of breath.

"I was there by Andy's side, he was still holding me. Well, holding my body anyway. That makes no sense, haven't I been here for days?"

"Time has no meaning here. There is no correlation between when you think you arrived and what is happening in the physical. Let's try something else," said Tilly as she tried to keep Laura engaged in a more pleasant activity. "Follow me."

Laura found herself standing at the front gate of a magnificent estate. Over the impressive iron-scrolled entrance hung the sign *Golden Aura Spa*. The two goddesses depicted in the scrollwork split as the gate opened to greet them. Inside, the array of flowers was spectacular. Tulips, Tilly's favorite, were bursting with color along the mosaic stone pathway. Further along, there were statues of all kinds in the garden. Laura particularly liked the one portraying several children playing on a teeter totter. A fawn appeared, as if to greet them, while a mother duck helped her young ones across the sparkling pond. Tilly gave her a broad smile as they entered. She knew that connecting with nature would help Laura to relax and feel more grounded in her new home.

"Another excellent feature of being here is learning that we are eternal, so I can look and feel any age I wish." And with that Tilly became a younger version of herself. She would have done it sooner if she thought Laura wouldn't freak out about it.

"Oh. How did you do that?" Laura was astonished at the change, but accepting of the transformation.

"Our self-concept determines our outer form."

"So, I can be whatever I want?"

"Yes. Just think it and it will be so."

"Then I wish to be Andy's bride." Tears welled up in her eyes, as she pictured herself with a bouquet of yellow tulips in her arms, pink and yellow ribbons trailing down the front of her long white dress. Andy wore a beige-linen suit with a yellow flower pinned to his lapel. She smiled as he reached for her hand when she approached the bow of the boat.

"Come back Laura." Tilly could see that she was drifting and needed to return her to the moment. She took her hands and led her down the walkway to their destination. At the inner entrance, Tilly placed her palm on the carved door, and it slowly opened inward toward the spa. She was greeted by the hostess, a small woman with a calming manner.

"Tilly, it is lovely to see you again. And you must be Laura. I am called Alicia." She held out both hands to welcome her new client.

"I've heard so much about you. How pretty you are. Tilly, you must be very proud. It must have been an exquisite flight." Her voice was more melodic than Laura could remember a voice to be. Her complexion glowed, almost sparkled. With short-cropped hair and tiny features, she had a pixie-like appearance. She motioned the pair inside with a graceful wave of her slender arm. Laura was sure she had never before seen the fabric that made up her flowing gold dress.

"It is an honor to have you join us on this most delightful day." Laura wondered if she meant at the spa or in this new world she found herself in. As picturesque as it was, she was not ready to be here. She just knew in her heart that her place was by Andy's side. There must be a way to get back to him.

"I expect that you will first wish to bathe in the pool of refreshment." And in response to Laura's confused expression, Alicia added some explanation. "This is the place and time for all past feeling to be at rest. The transition cannot be completed until you have been cleansed of all negative influence and washed of all remnants from your earthly experiences."

"But I don't want to lose the remnants of my earthly experiences," said Laura.

"Do not misunderstand. You will not forget. It will just ease your discomfort. You will be able to open yourself to receive this beautiful awareness, to become one with your soul."

"Sweetie, trust me. You'll feel terrific. I will never forget my first time. It really is soothing." Tilly gave herself a hug.

Laura reluctantly held out her hand and Alicia led her to an outdoor lake surrounded by rose bushes with fat blooms in every color she could imagine. The liquid was radiant, and as they entered the pool, it appeared to flow through and around their bodies. They swam to an iridescent-blue waterfall flowing with millions of tiny stars of light. Looking at one another, the two women laughed as points of radiant light passed through their bodies. They effortlessly moved to sit in a steam room that cleaned and brightened their auras.

"Please allow me to escort you next to the massage space. I believe you will find it most comforting." Alicia gently appeared and guided them into a lovely area that was bathed in soft, pink light. Exotic orchids filled the air with a fresh scent, and a melodic harp was playing in the background. Laura realized later that it was a trio of musicians playing in the adjacent courtyard.

"You will find a dressing gown there." She pointed to a closet door as tall as the room. Laura saw that there were two massage tables in the room, with a Japanese-style screen separating the two spaces for some privacy. She was becoming more relaxed with each activity.

"When you are ready, please ring the chime and your therapist will come in. Do you have any special requests?"

"I'll take Mario, if he's available." Tilly gave the hostess a sly grin, as she clutched her hands together.

"Tilly, for you, always." Alicia returned her grin.

"And Laura, I shall make the selection for your experience if that is acceptable . . ."

"Yes, I suppose that's fine." She put her trust in the woman she had just met.

When she left, Laura looked at Tilly and said "*Mario?*"

Tilly nodded and then stripped down on her side of the screen, anxiously looking forward to this treat. Laura was a bit more conservative and chose to cover herself with the soft, pink, Egyptian-cotton sheet. As she lay on the table she closed her eyes to relax for the first time since she had arrived in this astral world. Laura had to admit that the silent masseuse had magic hands. Her skin had never felt so soft after being oiled with a sweet vanilla lotion. Every part of her body was totally stress-free as though she was finally beginning to release her attachment to it. She turned to thank her therapist, but was surprised to see that no one was in the room.

Tilly thanked Mario and said goodbye with a sexy innuendo, but Laura never saw a man leave the room. Could it be? She had so much to learn here.

"So tell me. Tilly. Did we create that, too? Even Mario?"

"Now you're catching on. Lessons don't have to be hard or boring. Besides, why have just anyone give me a massage when I can have Mario, my very own perfect design?"

When they had put on their robes, Alicia came into the room.

"Ladies, I trust that you enjoyed your experience?" Alicia didn't need an answer to her question.

After what seemed like hours of pure and radiant pampering, they had one final activity. They entered a perfectly round room that had what looked like tuning forks stationed around the perimeter of the entire room. Sitting in the very center of the room, back to back, Laura and Tilly listened as the forks began to correspond with each other in lyrical tones of music. The harmonizing affect was seen clearly as Laura watched their chakras resonate and change colors to the different sounds.

As they walked from the spa they absolutely glowed. Both appeared noticeably younger and completely rejuvenated. They glanced at each other and laughed like schoolgirl friends as they exited the spa.

"Bye Alicia. We'll be back soon." Tilly waved.

"Nice to meet you, Alicia. Thanks again, it was amazing." Laura meant it.

"It was truly my pleasure," responded Alicia, as always grateful to be a part of this process where one's soul was opened to receive the inner light. She watched as the two ladies walked down the lane, eventually out of her sight.

"Tilly, that was a beautiful experience, but I still don't understand why I am here. It seems like I should be comfortable by now, but I just can't seem to adjust."

Tilly brought her back to the cottage and led her to a small pond surrounded by lush vegetation. Weeping Willow trees were at one side and brilliant-red Japanese maples were directly facing them. She tossed a pebble into the pond making concentric circles in the water.

"See how the water ripples out in all directions when the pebble hits the water?" Tilly asked.

"Yes," answered Laura without lifting her head.

"Each event in life causes the same effect. No matter where the pebble lands in the water, or how big the pebble is, there is always the same reaction in the water."

"So, you're saying that my being here is linked to a chain of events?" Laura was becoming interested.

"Exactly, and the chain of events will continue. Every individual is on earth to learn and we cannot get in the way of that plan, as it would interfere with the soul's personal evolution. This is why we shouldn't attempt to influence the ripple. Sometimes it's not easy to grow, but we learn from challenges. There are no short cuts. We learn by being," said Tilly in a rare moment of serious dialogue.

Laura followed the garden path around the pond appreciating the colors and combinations that formed small bouquets along the trail. Out across the field a panorama of flowers gently swayed in the breeze. Tilly moved to the center of her stone labyrinth and turned as she continued to enhance her sprawling garden of exotic flowers. She was designing colorful combinations of hybrid tulips, orange dahlias, white hyacinths, and lilacs because she felt the need to reinforce the concepts of creation.

"Tilly, they are so beautiful."

"As is the system in which we find ourselves."

"So what's next? In this system that you describe," asked Laura.

"I think you are ready," Tilly said as they had their morning tea on the porch.

"Ready? Ready for what?" Laura was unwilling to commit to this new environment and still a little hesitant to venture beyond her world with Tilly. It was an intuitive feeling that her next step would be permanent and she would never be able to return to her beloved.

"This," and with a dramatic swirl of light Tilly carried Laura to a school playground.

Outside playing in the sunshine of the clear blue sky, there were children lined up at the stairs to a sliding board. Some boys were laughing and kicking a soccer ball around on a grass play area. Still others were making mini-sculptures in the sand box. Laughter and joy filled the air around them. Tilly and Laura stood by the playground at the entrance to the school. Chimes played softly in the background and Laura watched as the young residents started to line up at the door.

"I thought you might like to visit this place," Tilly said as she gestured toward the building.

"A school! Full of children!" Laura was fascinated.

"There are lots of schools here. Many of these children crossed over at a very young age and need special assistance. You are a wonderful teacher and you may choose to teach again here."

"Yes, that sounds perfect! Can we go inside?" Laura asked.

Laura and Tilly followed them into the fairy-tale structure, where the classrooms were now full of children, bathed in beams of natural light that bounced off of the colorful accessories. In the corner was an older woman playing the piano. A picture of Laura's student, Ashley, was framed and displayed there. The woman nodded in Laura's direction, and she gave a little wave back.

Several of the students looked up at the pair and waved or smiled. Laura went into one of the classrooms to get a better look. Inside there were several desks where children were creating art projects or putting puzzles together. One child sat alone reading. Laura approached the child and knelt down to his level.

"Hi, there. My name's Laura. What are you reading?"

"The Pokey Puppy. It's my favorite book. I got it for my birthday," said the little boy.

"I remember that story. I used to read it to my students," and with that thought, Laura felt like now was her chance to return to the world she had left so abruptly.

"Tilly," said Laura as she stood and turned to her guardian.

"Yes, dear."

"I can't thank you enough for all you have done, all you have taught me. I truly appreciate the insight you've shared with me, but I know in my heart that I don't belong here. Whatever it takes, I'm going back," said Laura. She felt that her time was running out and that if she was to return it had to be now.

"That is a serious decision, one that only you and your higher self can make. But I know you will choose wisely," said Tilly, knowing that this was a choice over which she had no influence.

"Andy loves and needs me, my students will miss me, and I have a physical life that I need to see through."

"Well then, if you are sure then you must go."

After a quick kiss goodbye on Tilly's cheek, Laura looked up, stretched her arms to the side and said, "Now I am back to the physical world!" Tilly waved as Laura's form disintegrated before her eyes.

"Take care, my sweetheart. When you are ready to come back and stay, I'll be here waiting for you. And so will these sweet school kids." Tilly was not surprised at her decision to reunite with the physical, but it was so rare that someone could make it happen she couldn't help but feel a swell of pride at the strength Laura had developed since she arrived.

Andy bent one last time to kiss the love of his life. He gently placed his lips on hers, tasting the salt from his own tears that had fallen onto her tranquil face. The pain in his chest was unbearable, as he believed his life had ended with hers. In a very subtle movement, he felt her lips respond. Could it be real? He leaned back and watched in pure joy as Laura's eyes blinked open. She squeezed Andy's hand, which had not let go since he first lifted her from the street. The EMT shouted to the driver, "She's back! Let's get moving!"

"Laura. Oh thank God. I thought you'd left us."

"Andy, I couldn't leave you. We have so much to do, to live for," said Laura as she struggled to get the words out. Silently she again thanked her Aunt Tilly for all that she had learned, knowing that her lessons would be important in the coming days of her physical life.

"You are more than welcome my dear. I know that you'll make a beautiful bride." Tilly would miss her, but had to admit she was anxious to move on with her own astral life. Now that Laura had safely returned to Andy, Tilly could begin to consider her next move.

"I guess Mario can help me with that!"

THE POWER OF THE KEY

Shifting on the cold bench seat trying to find a comfortable or even bearable position, Quinn tapped one foot on the broken-tiled floor. Checking again and again for his wallet and car keys, he felt like these few simple acts were the only thing he could control. The air was heavy, dark, and dusty, so thick with haze that he could barely see in front of him. The outlines of human form were shuffling around in circles with their heads held low. It seemed natural to absorb the sadness in this place; the confusion and sense of loss waved through him.

Not sure how or when he got here, he tried to remember the words that he had heard so many years ago. "Awareness Now!" He said it first to himself, almost in a whisper. Feeling stronger, he stood and shouted with raised arms, "Awareness Now!" He demanded it and would accept nothing less.

In an immediate contrast to the previous environment, a shiny cream-colored limousine pulled up close to the curb. As the rear window silently slid down, a middle-aged woman in a white business suit called out to him. "Hello. My name is Akari and I'm here for you." Even though the voice was slightly familiar, he looked around to see who the passenger might be addressing.

"Yes, I'm talking to you Quinn." she opened the back door, and reached out to take his hands, gently guiding him to a seat next to her. The car was clean and cool, filled with fresh air and an ever so slight scent of sandalwood. The deep, plush seat cradled him and he felt safe, at peace for the first time in recent memory.

"I need to show you a few things before we can get to your destination," she said as the car began to move forward.

"And you are . . . ?" Quinn asked her.

"You asked for awareness, did you not? It is my job to assist," Akari assured him when Quinn nodded in agreement.

He wasn't sure why, but Quinn trusted this woman without hesitation. Relaxing his tired body against the luxurious headrest, he decided that he would go along with whatever she directed him to do.

"Your first stop is a party," she said as she opened the door for him. "Go on. Join them if you'd like."

Quinn stepped out of the car and onto a lawn where dozens of people were talking and laughing over inside jokes. Some lively jazz played in the background and the clinking glasses created a festive atmosphere. It was contagious and Quinn felt at home, grabbing a champagne flute from one of the long tables. Under the fairy lights, he saw Akari watching him. The lights cleared his vision so he had a better view. As his sight became stronger, Quinn could see that no one was moving from their current position.

"Why? Why are they so fixed at a single location? There is no mingling, no wandering from one group to another. This seems strange," he thought.

"Move closer." Akari's voice was clear in his head.

Only then did he notice each of the party goers had a chain around their ankle. Quinn thought they must be inmates of some kind.

"You would be correct, but not in the prison that you would expect."

As Quinn's sight became even sharper, he saw writing on each shackle. The words were surprising to him. There was *Career* on one, *Family Home* on another, and *Social Media* on a third. He moved quietly through the crowd seeing *Alcoholic* and *Gambler* in deep conversation. He confirmed that every person there had an attachment that was binding them to the spot on the ground where they stood. *Car Collection* and *Political Party* became visible. This was so clear to him now. All of these people were welded to a spot, unable to move because of their attachment, their role, their self-identity.

Quinn looked at one woman whose attachment said *Health Fanatic*. He approached her to ask about it.

"Yes, I am totally committed to having a healthy body. I eat organic, exercise every day, yoga twice per week, and wear natural fabrics," she replied, proud of her focus and success.

"Well that sounds reasonable and practical, Akari. What is the problem with that?" asked Quinn.

"That was a valuable practice when she was an Earth being. But it is not relevant now. She is so conditioned to believe that she is her body that she continues to nurture a physical form that is no longer present."

"You also see that each has a cord around their neck that holds a key." Akari pointed out to him.

On one key was the phrase *Self-Awareness*, and *Enlightenment* was on another. *Higher Self* and *Inner Consciousness* were glowing words on some keys, but it seemed that no one was looking in that direction. Instinctively, Quinn knew that each of these people could unlock their position at any time simply by invoking the power of the key.

"Use your key!" Quinn said loudly as he tried unsuccessfully to move through the crowd. "The key will unlock your shackle. You'll be free." Few acknowledged his suggestion and even fewer actually looked down at their attachments. They seemed happy to stay just as they were.

"Before you judge, perhaps you should look at your own attachment. You are also stagnant." Akari pointed to Quinn's ankle where he saw the same chain that had been so prevalent at the party. "Like those on the lawn, as long as you focus your energy on the physical you can never be free to explore the path to your true self-awareness." Quinn looked at his own ankle and saw *Money Obsession.*

"I buy lottery tickets and make an occasional visit to the casino. That's no big deal, somebody is going to win all that cash and it might just as well be me."

Akari tilted her head sideways and looked at him and sent him a thought. "Is that all you want to acknowledge?"

"Yes, I have a Jaguar, but everyone in my neighborhood drives a nice car. And I think I deserve a big house because I've worked hard all my life to earn it. I don't see a problem here," Quinn said as he unconsciously adjusted the TAG Heuer Chronograph watch on his wrist.

"It is not merely the objects that you describe. It is how you associate money with success that makes it difficult to release. Letting go of your relentless pursuit of wealth and expensive material things will reveal your true net worth. You can do it. Use your key," encouraged Akari as she pointed to the cord around his neck.

The key said *Detachment,* and reluctantly Quinn placed it into his lock and found that he became lighter with more freedom of movement.

"Are you ready for more?" Akari asked.

"Yes."

They both returned to the car and with a knock on the dividing glass, they began to move forward until a crowd of human forms standing in the road forced them to stop. They stood in a circle with their backs to the middle. Some were crying, others appeared to be angry, a few were laughing at the ones who were in distress. Some were just staring out into space.

"What's wrong with them? Why don't they move so I can continue my journey?" Quinn asked as he opened the door and got out of the car.

"They all have a connection to you," Akari explained when she joined him. "Look closely at each of their faces." She gave Quinn a moment to study the group.

"I do see," he answered. "There are my first wife, my mother, and a school friend. Why are they here? What do they want?"

"Your wife needs forgiveness for the path she took that ended your marriage. She cannot leave this circle until you allow her to move away from it. Next to her is a former co-worker who has always regretted taking credit for the project you worked on together. He got promoted, you ended up quitting the firm, and that changed the direction of your life. He never knew what happened to you. He needs closure," said Akari as she pointed around the circle.

"And there is my sister who helped to raise me when my mother became ill. I am so grateful that she put her life on hold so that I did not go to the home of a stranger. I don't think I ever truly thanked her for that."

"It isn't too late to tell her that you are grateful. You can thank her now," said Akari.

"Thank you Marianne. I never told you how your selflessness changed my life. I love you."

And as Quinn talked to his sister, she became covered in a glowing light and was released. She smiled and began to float away from the group.

"Yes, it can be just that easy," Akari assured him. "Would you like to try another?"

"Jane. You were my wife for just a few years. They were good years and I was just as much to blame for our short time together. You were strong to follow your path and because you left, I was forced to become more independent. I wouldn't have led the life I had if we had stayed together. But if you are looking for forgiveness, I will give it."

With a glow of light emanating from her heart chakra, Jane rose above the circle and dissipated into a green mist. One by one, each person spoke to Quinn and faded away from the circle.

"Why were they waiting?"

"You could not move forward on your path until you had provided resolution with each of these beings. They also required something from you before they could progress. You have given them freedom as well as opened the way for yourself."

"What if I had not come this way? Would they have remained here until I had spoken with them?"

"If you had not resolved these emotional entanglements, you would find yourself back in similar situations later in this life—or even beyond, into your next lives. It's all about learning through experience, acknowledging the role each soul plays in your life."

Quinn was feeling pretty good about this process so far. It made sense to him now, all of it. The only question that remained was where and how this drive would end. He was content with the lessons he had gathered so far. But what would be next? The thought made him uncomfortable, even fearful.

With that thought, the car came to an abrupt halt as the driver slammed on the brakes.

"What is it?" Quinn called to the driver. "Why the sudden stop?" Even though he remained invisible through the blackened glass, he was hoping the chauffer had heard him.

"Well, let's take a look." Akari offered her hand once again as she opened the door for him.

It only took a moment for Quinn to see it. A massive presence stood in front of the car. Covered with matted brown fur, the creature was so tall that it cast a shadow across the hood. The hairy, muscular arms rose and waved angrily. But it was the beast's roar that thawed Quinn's frozen stance; a thunderous bellow hit his face so hard, it knocked him back a step.

"He is your creation," Akari said as Quinn tried to get back into the car. "And as such, only you can send him away."

"How am I supposed to do that? He is terrifying—bigger, stronger, and louder than me."

"Is he?" Akari gently pushed him forward, closer to the creature.

Knowing this was part of the planned experience, Quinn asked, "Do you have suggestions on how I can do it? How I can rid myself of this overwhelming monster?"

The brute looked him in the eyes, as though he was waiting for Quinn's response. At that moment, Quinn knew. Sending beams of unconditional love, he held out his arms to this being and moved forward to hug him. The embrace was returned and the beast that had been so intimidating shrunk to the size of a puppy.

"Your fear," Akari said.

"My fear?"

"Yes. You expressed fear-based thoughts and they manifested as you pictured them."

"And when I embraced my fear, it dissolved into something that would no longer stand in my way."

"Exactly. And now that you have addressed the last of your challenges, your opportunity to move higher awaits."

"Opportunity? To move higher?" Quinn asked. "I don't understand."

"Step back into the car and I will show you." Akari waved her arm toward the back door and it opened. He climbed in as he had done so many times before, but rather than entering the interior of a car, Quinn found himself walking into an entirely different environment.

He was not in the car at all, but on a grassy field at the base of a small hill. The sun was shining brightly, creating a perfect, warm day. The smell of sandalwood from the car was replaced by the fragrance wafting from the lavender fields on his right.

"Start here," Akari said, pointing to a smooth path. "When you get to the top, keep climbing. You will encounter this opening many more times, so practice your ascent as often as you can. You can now go as high as you wish—up into the clouds and beyond."

He was ready but had just one bit of curiosity left. He stood still and asked the question that had been on his mind since they met at the bus stop: "Who are you?"

"I am you, a part of your inner being that knows you and loves you. I will always support you, never leave you. I am the light within."

"And the driver?"

Akari just nodded because she knew Quinn had the answer already in his heart.

"That is also me," he stopped to clarify in his mind, "because I am the driver of my thoughts and actions. I have personal responsibility for what happens in this life and the next."

"You are right. The power is always within your grasp," and with that Akari and all of the surrounding scenery began to fade away.

As he started to regain control of his arms and legs, Quinn sat up from his position on the leather couch in his massive home office. From this position, he could not help but see the possessions he had accumulated. There were shelves, glass cases, and ornate boxes—all filled with the expensive novelties he had collected through the years. Good investments, he was told.

He had an unfamiliar but confident feeling that all that surrounded him was a façade of the being that he really was—trappings of a human who valued physical things over spiritual development. He knew what he had to do next, and just by making that decision, Quinn was finally free to focus on what was truly of real and lasting importance.

OTHER BOOKS BY WILLIAM BUHLMAN

Adventures Beyond the Body

This classic bestselling book on out-of-body experiences demonstrates how to project consciousness outside the limits of the physical body, sharing Buhlman's own journey and providing simple techniques for readers to use in pursuit of their spiritual evolution. Astral travel can not only expand your consciousness but also verify the existence of the soul, teach you about past lives, and enhance your daily life.

The Secret of the Soul

This book is an extensive examination into the out-of-body experience as it relates to the nature of reality, filled with over two hundred experiences obtained from 16,000 survey responses from people all over the world. The techniques that accompany the examples will assist you in attaining profound transformation in your awareness.

Adventures in the Afterlife

After a terminal illness takes the life of the main character, Frank Brooks, the reader is treated to an uplifting spiritual journey into multiple realities and spiritual-training environments existing within the afterlife. This compelling story is followed by valuable information and strategic-planning tools to make the afterlife journey an exciting and spiritually rewarding adventure.

Higher Self Now!

This is a modern guidebook for personal transformation focused on the continuation of the soul after physical death. Learning how to navigate thought-responsive realities clears the way for you to achieve escape velocity. This book is complemented with the true accounts of those who are nearing death by William's wife, Susan, an end-of-life doula, who adds her observations, clarifications, and suggestions for assisting your loved ones through this transitional experience that we call death.

AUDIO PRODUCTS BY WILLIAM BUHLMAN

Out-of-Body Techniques (with Hemi-Sync®)

A six-CD set that includes a variety of full-length techniques for out-of-body travel. Each is supported by Hemi-Sync® technology and an instruction manual to assist you in your out-of-body practice. An instructional PDF is available for the digital product, located at www.astralinfo.org.

Destination: Higher Self! (with Hemi-Sync®)

A two-CD set with three gentle meditations that are designed to support you and your loved ones during transition. This set includes Hemi-Sync®. Instructions are provided to help you release personal fears and attachments while embracing the unlimited freedom of the spiritual self. This set is designed to be used with the book Higher Self Now!

How to Have an Out-of-Body Experience

Produced by: *Sounds True*

This is a practical six-CD course for entering and navigating out-of-body experiences, teaching you how to extend your consciousness and quicken your inner spiritual unfolding. With almost seven hours of instruction and techniques, this set helps you explore the subtle realms with safety and confidence.

For more information go to www.astralinfo.org.

You will find:

- Upcoming Events
- Audio Products
- OBE Techniques
- Spiritual Directive Instructions
- Keys to Control
- Share your Experience
- Methods to Control Fear
- Frequently Asked Questions

.... and much more.

WILLIAM BUHLMAN

The author's forty years of extensive personal out-of-body explora-tions give him a unique and thought provoking insight. His first book, Adventures beyond the Body chronicles his personal journey of self-discovery through out-of-body travel, and provides the reader with the preparation and techniques that can be used for their own adventure.

Over the past three decades William has developed an effective system to experience safe, self-initiated out-of-body adventures. He conducts an in-depth workshop titled, Out-of-Body Exploration Intensive at the renowned Monroe Institute in Virginia. As a certified hypnotherapist, William incorporates various methods, including hypnosis, visualization and meditation techniques in his workshops to explore the profound nature of out-of-body experiences and the benefits of accelerated personal development. Through lectures, workshops and his books the author teaches the preparation and techniques of astral projection and spiritual exploration.

The author brings a refreshing look to how we can use out-of-body experiences to explore our spiritual identity and enhance our intellectual and physical lives. William is best known for his ability to teach people how to have profound spiritual adventures through the use of out-of-body experiences and altered states of consciousness. In addition, he has developed an extensive series of audio programs that are designed to expand awareness and assist in the exploration of consciousness. William has appeared on a variety of radio, television, and YouTube shows worldwide.

William's books are currently available in twelve languages. The author lives in the USA. For more information visit the author's web site, www.astralinfo.org.

SUSAN BUHLMAN

Susan Buhlman is a hospice volunteer and a certified end-of-life doula.
It is her passion and her soul's purpose to provide comfort to those who are
actively dying. As a companion to those in the final hours or days of life,
she offers a calming, compassionate presence and, if the patient is open
to it, Susan guides him or her through a transitional preparation process.
Guided visualizations, positive affirmations, Hemi-Sync® and energy
healing are a few of the tools that are used to ease the emotional pain
and fear of the dying process. As a coach during bereavement workshops,
she uses spiritual principles to lessen the burden of loss, leading the way
toward a peaceful appreciation of the next conscious steps in our soul's
journey. For more information visit www.astralinfo.org.

ACKNOWLEDGMENTS

We appreciate all who have participated in our workshops over the years. Whether it was residential or online the dedication to enhancing your journey of consciousness has been an inspiration.

We truly value the fine editing skills and thoughtful comments provided by our friend Claudia Carlton Lambright (cclediting@gmail.com). As always it was great working with you.

Block of Ice is dedicated to Carlos. Thank you for your service to our country and—through this story—for your service to all who are frozen.

―――――

Because there are so many individuals and experiences that impact our journey, we invite the readers to share in our *Moment of Gratitude*:

I am grateful for this day knowing that all events and people have been placed before me as lessons. I am reminded that all things happen for my highest good, to enrich my life journey, and create awareness on my evolutionary path.